PATTERNS IN
MORAL
DEVELOPMENT
Revised

Catherine M. Stonehouse
Foreword by Ted Ward

Wipf and Stock Publishers
150 West Broadway • Eugene OR 97401
2000

Patterns in Moral Development

By Stonehouse, Catherine M.
Copyright©1980 by Stonehouse, Catherine M.
ISBN: 1-57910-625-0

Reprinted by *Wipf and Stock Publishers*
150 West Broadway • Eugene OR 97401

Previously published by Word Publications, 1980.

To my father who . . .

> *introduced me to the world of ideas,*
> *explored with me the principles of God's Word,*
> *was alongside in my struggles of faith,*
> *and provided an atmosphere of love and respect*
> *in which I could grow.*

Contents

Foreword by Ted Ward

Foreword

The Word of God is concerned with the moral development of humanity. Making men and women righteous in the sight of God is at the heart of God's great redemptive acts. The Bible teaches that it is only through the redeeming blood of Jesus Christ that sinful humanity can be made right before God. Thus the issue of being "saved" or "lost" depends on faith in Jesus Christ. But God's whole redemptive plan for the creation involves far more. What is the process through which one's conscience develops? What happens as a child learns the difference between right and wrong? Why is it that among all of us-Christians and non-Christians alike-that there are acts of kindness and acts of selfish evil? Other than religious decisions and commitments, what are the values that underlie moral behavior? Where do they come from? How do they develop?

Just a few years ago the Lilly Endowment gave Michigan State University a substantial grant to gather a research team and seek a better understanding of these questions. Our task was to examine the twentieth century research, especially in social science, that deals with moral and ethical judgment and the processes by which people's values develop. We were to carry out research on the *research*, to discover the practical implications. We focused on four matters: what every person ought to know about what goes on inside oneself as moral values are put into action, what part the parent can play in the development of a child's moral judgment, what part teachers and schools can play, and what part religious education can play.

Catherine Stonehouse was a deeply respected member of that research team. One of many outcomes of her service with us was the original manuscript for this book. She poured herself into it, so great was her concern for effective home and church influence on the lives of boys and girls. She went into many church education conferences and seminars to test the early version of the material. Nothing less than the best would satisfy Cathy.

In the chapters that follow, we have the highlights of those efforts. Making research interesting isn't always successful. But there are pleasant surprises ahead in this book. You will find practical yet thoroughly responsible answers to the question, "What can I do that will help children and young people in their moral judgment?" As an additional bonus, you will surely get some new insights into yourself-what goes on in your judgmental processes as you make moral choices, and how you came to be the person that you are.

Dr. Stonehouse is dealing with difficult material. She handles it in interesting yet thorough ways. Her years of experience engaged in strengthening the effectiveness of Sunday school volunteers and Christian education staff show through on every page.

Try to learn from this book. Reading it is not enough. As you come to the end of each short section there are questions to be answered. On the basis of what you have read, try to answer them for yourself. In doing so you will be able to remember and put into practice far more of the valuable information in this book.

Ted Ward
Professor of Curriculum Research
Michigan State University

1.

PATTERNS IN MORAL DEVELOPMENT

Hard questions jump out at us from the pages of our magazines and newspapers. "Is Keeping People Alive Unethical?" * When there seems to be no hope of recovery and life is being sustained only by the use of machines, does a person have the right to be allowed to die? Who should make such decisions? On what grounds? These are questions that were not a problem thirty or forty years ago. Modern technology has brought us many lifesaving devices, but with them have come troubling moral questions. Are we preparing our children, youth, and adults to deal with these difficult moral questions?

Our world is complex and rapidly changing. Many moral standards once supported through social pressure are no longer accepted by many in the society. At high school or college, and on the job young people will have their moral standards and judgments questioned. Will they know the reason for their beliefs and be prepared to stand against the crowd?

And what do our students do when they meet a new situation for which they have no rule of right conduct? Have we helped them to discover the principles behind rules of conduct, principles that can be applied in many new situations? Christian educators and parents are deeply concerned about these questions. They want to do the best job possible to help persons develop morally.I

In recent years important research has been conducted in the area of moral development. Christian scholars have taken the findings of this research and examined them in the light of God's Word. The harmony between the findings of researchers such as Lawrence Kohlberg and the glimpses of moral development given in God's Word is exciting.

This book has been designed to introduce you to the pattern of moral development which scientists see as they study human beings, God's greatest creation. We will also look at the factors which are at work as moral reasoning develops. After exploring these processes of moral development we will turn our attention to the role of parents and teachers in moral development. What can we do to facilitate the development of the children, youth, or adults with whom we work? We will begin to answer this question by discovering some of the components of an atmosphere that is most healthy for development. In the final chapter we will discuss the kinds of experiences and support which we can provide to enhance development.

And now, let us look at some general understandings about our students, "What Makes Them Tick"; their moral judgments, "The Reason Behind the Answer"; and the pattern they will follow in the development of their moral reasoning, "Levels of Moral Development."

---

* *Eternity,* February 1976.

WHAT MAKES THEM TICK?

There is no simple answer to the question, "What makes them tick?" Human beings are complex. To understand them we must think of each person as a complex whole of interacting parts. More than just physical bodies, people are also thoughts, feelings, and actions. We talk about what people know, feel, and do. Knowing, feeling, and doing are interrelated factors which influence each other. A person who has been deeply hurt by a Christian may develop bitter feelings toward Christians. These feelings may cause the person to hear only negative things that are said about Christianity. Feelings influence what we know because they create barriers which keep us from hearing certain things and cause us to want to learn more about other things. New knowledge however, may cause attitudes and feelings to change. Carrying out certain actions helps us gain new knowledge about ourselves and the things we're working with. Behaving in new ways may also bring about changes in attitudes and feelings. On the other hand, new knowledge and attitudes may cause behavior change. As we try to help students learn we must remember that knowing, feeling, or doing cannot be separated from each other. Learning involves the complex interaction of all these factors.

The human mind is not an empty box which admits more and more information. The human mind is active. It works with and organizes the information which it receives. The result of this organizing is a certain perspective or way of looking at things and making judgments. The mind is not a mirror which passively and accurately reflects the outside world. The mind is more like an artist who paints a personal interpretation of what he or she sees.[1] A person's way of viewing or interpreting the world goes through a process of development. The six-year-old understands the world in a way that is very different from most sixteen-year-olds. We say that they are at different levels of development. But every sixteen-year-old at one time interpreted the world as the six-year-old does now. This is so because each person follows a similar pattern as he or she develops through the various levels of moral reasoning.

It seems that God has designed humans to go through a long process of development. We see this in the physical realm. A human baby develops physical skills much more slowly than a puppy. No amount of effort on the part of parents will cause a child to learn to walk before he or she is ready. But through this slow process of development, humans reach far beyond the abilities of the animals which develop much more quickly.

Experience has taught us to accept the speed at which physical development occurs. But we tend to think that we can make mental and moral development happen in a child as quickly as we like, if we-the teachers and parents-know the right things to do. But slow development following a certain pattern seems to be God's design for humans in regard to the mental and the moral as well as the physical. In the area of moral development certain ways of understanding the world and making moral judgments must be mastered before one is ready to move on to higher, more adequate interpretations of what is right or wrong. As we will see in the pages that follow, moral development is a lifelong process. Persons can and should be continually involved in the process of

---

[1] David Elkind gives us the mirror/artist analogy in his very helpful book, *Children and Adolescents: Interpretive Essays on Jean Piaget* (New York, London, Toronto: Oxford University Press, 1974).

developing, but the path to the higher levels of moral reasoning is a long one.

Time Out!

Although we have not answered the question, "What makes them tick?" we have suggested a few things that should be kept in mind when trying to answer that question.

From the statements below choose those which you think are in line with the preceding discussion.

A. To understand learning and developing we must think of the person as a complex whole made up of interacting parts.
B. The mind is like a mirror which accurately reflects reality.
C. Moral development can be greatly speeded up if adults working with children know the right things to do.

Did you choose "A"? If so, you are doing fine. A person can only be understood when seen as a complex, dynamic whole. Each part of the person affects each other part.

The mind is not a passive mirror but an active artist. Statement "B" is therefore incorrect. Two persons may observe the same event but interpret it very differently. As we develop we come to view and interpret the world in new ways. We use different levels of reasoning.

Development is a slow process. We do not help the child by trying to make development happen more quickly than what is natural. Statement "C" suggests that teachers and parents concerned about moral development should learn the right things to do so that they can speed it up. Such efforts will not be fruitful. Teachers and parents can, however, learn how to work with natural processes and facilitate moral development. That's what this book is all about.

THE REASON BEHIND THE ANSWER

In many places on a Sunday morning you could find teachers telling the story of a child facing a moral dilemma. To test the moral judgment of the students the teacher asks, "Now what should Johnny do?" If the children respond with, "Johnny should tell the truth, be nice to the new boy, or help the old lady," the teacher smiles, says "*Very* good" and goes merrily on thinking that the children are developing sound moral judgment. But are they? Why did Mark, Susan, and Tom give the answers they did? Unless the teacher knows the reasoning behind the answers no judgment can be made about the level of the child's moral development.

Moral judgment has two components: content-the answer given to the "What should Johnny do?" question; and structure-the reasoning process that led the person to decide on a certain solution to a moral dilemma.

[2] In the church we have been concerned about what people ought to do-the content of moral judgments. That is important. But we have often not given adequate attention to the reasons for moral action.

---

[2] The following titles are included for those who wish to read more from Kohlberg's work.

Kohlberg, Lawrence (with Philip Whitten) "Understanding the Hidden Curriculum" *Learning*, December 1972.

Kohlberg, Lawrence "A Cognitive-Developmental Approach to Moral Education" *The Humanist*, November/December 1972.

Kohlberg, Lawrence *Collected Papers on Moral Development and Education* (Cambridge: Laboratory of Human Development, 1973).

The same content or solution might be suggested by persons at very different levels of moral maturity. But the reasons for their solution will differ greatly. One child might reason, "Johnny should tell the truth because if he lies his mother will find out and he will get a spanking." Another child's thinking might run along these lines, "Johnny should tell the truth because if he does God will be pleased with him, and so will his mother." We have here examples of two different levels of moral judgment. It is the structure-the why or the reasoning-that gives the clue as to a person's level of development.

The structure of moral reasoning determines how a person hears moral messages. When we hear new moral reasoning that is just beyond us, we are attracted to it and this helps us develop. But if the new reasoning is much above us, we distort it. We make it fit into our own way of thinking and do not realize that we were introduced to something new. The structures of the mind-the way of reasoning-must develop if persons are to be able to comprehend mature moral judgments.

Time Out!

Which of the following statements indicates the structure of the person's moral judgment?

A. Cindy should not tell on her sister, because she might want her sister to keep a secret for her sometime.
B. Cindy should tell her parents everything that happened.

If you chose "A" you are right. "A" gives the reason for the decision which indicates the structure of the judgment. "B" merely gives the solution or content with no clues as to the reasoning that has led to the answer.

Which sentence is content and which is structure?

A. The boy who broke five glasses helping his mother is naughtier than the boy who broke one glass climbing on the cupboard to get a cookie.
B. Five glasses is more than one. So breaking five is naughtier than breaking one.

The "B" sentence represents the structure because it gives the reasoning behind the answer.

Which statement helps the teacher know the level of moral development of the student?

A. Kevin should not smoke because if he gets caught he will be kicked off the team.
B. Kevin should not smoke because a good athlete will keep the training rules. If he is a good athlete he must do what good athletes do.

Both "A" and "B" give the teacher clues as to the development of the student's moral reasoning. Both responses show the same solution or content- Kevin should not smoke. But the reasons given for not smoking indicate judgments coming from two different structures of thinking. The decisions are based on different perspectives of what is considered right and wrong.

LEVELS OF MORAL DEVELOPMENT

In the 1920's a man by the name of Jean Piaget began a life long study of children. He made some fascinating discoveries about the moral judgments of children. As he talked with them he found that their judgments were very different from those of adults. He noted interesting characteristics of thinking that showed up in children of different ages.

Kohlberg was interested in the judgments which Piaget described. He decided to explore the area of moral development further. In the late fifties he began to study the development of moral reasoning in a group of some seventy boys. During a thirty year time span, every three years, Kohlberg has again interviewed these boys--now men. From this long term study and other studies in several different cultures, Kohlberg has identified three levels in the development of moral reasoning. His research indicates that all persons work through these levels of development in the same order. The speed of development and the final level reached varies from person to person, but the sequence is always the same.

Before looking at the characteristics of the three levels let us define a little more clearly what is meant by a level of moral reasoning. Each level is characterized by reasoning that is of a different quality than that used at the other levels. We will find that at each level persons have a different understanding of right and wrong. They have different reasons for doing right. The quality of their moral reasoning changes from level to level. Development from one level to the next calls for a major rearranging of one's thinking; a more comprehensive and refined way of viewing and understanding life.

Each level of development is important. It seems that the way of thinking used at each level is essential preparation for the new dimensions of reasoning at the next level. Since each new level builds on the preceding one, no level can be skipped. The only way to get to level three from level one is to work through level two. For this reason there is a similar pattern to the development of moral reasoning for all persons.

Time Out!

Which of these statements do you think is true?

A. The three levels of moral reasoning differ mainly in the amount of knowledge the learner has acquired by the time he or she reaches the level.
B. Moral development is different for each individual. You will find very few persons for whom the path of moral development is in any way similar.
C. All persons work through the levels of moral reasoning in the same order. Individuals do differ, however, in the rate of their development and the highest level they reach.

What was your choice? "C"? Good.

Learning new facts and adding new ideas to concepts is part of the process of development, but levels of moral reasoning differ mainly in the quality of thinking used. Therefore, statement "A" is wrong.

Statements "B" and "C" present contrasting views of development. Contrary to "B," research indicates that there is a universal pattern of moral development. The sequence for working through the stages of moral reasoning is the same for all persons (C). But development is not identical for everyone. Persons develop at different rates. A few adults do not develop beyond level one, others stay at level two.

Moving On

But what do these levels of moral reasoning look like? Let's explore that question now.

LEVELS OF MORAL DEVELOPMENT

Kohlberg refers to the three levels of moral development as: I) Preconventional, 11) Conventional, and 111) Postconventional or Principled. Conventional has to do with what society in general believes to be right. We might describe the Preconventional Level as including persons who are not yet able to understand and apply the moral rules of the general society. Persons at the Conventional Level live in accordance with the moral standards of their friends and society. At the Postconventional Level persons can go beyond the rules of the society. They understand principles that can be applied in situations where moral conflict occurs or where there are no set rules of conduct.

To be more specific, at the Preconventional Level, children are aware of some of the rules in their world. They know many of the things to which the labels good and bad are attached. Their attention, however, is focused on the physical results of an action or the pleasure that is likely to come from the act. Punishment, rewards, and the exchange of favors play a large part in the child's moral judgments. The physical power of the person who gives a rule or labels something good or bad, influences the way a child feels about the rule or label.

Conventional level persons are interested in maintaining the expectations of their family, friends, and society, This is more important to them than the immediate results of an action. The commitment to the expectations goes beyond mere conformity to the standards. Conventional persons have a sense of loyalty to the social order. They support, maintain, and defend it.

They identify strongly with other persons of their group, believing that their way is the right way.

Another way of labeling the levels of development is with reference to the source of authorities to which the person looks when judging right and wrong. The source of authority for level one is self-interest. Level two persons look to external standards and those at level three to internal principles. The levels could therefore be labeled: I. Level of self-interest, II. Level of external standards, III. Level of internal principles.

The Premoral Level

Kohlberg identifies a level prior to level one, the premoral period of life. Prior to the age of five or six, children do not have the maturity of thought to consider a moral dilemma and make a judgment based on what is just or fair. They do what they want or what seems best from their perspective--what will bring pleasure or avoid pain without thought as to whether it is right or wrong. Their actions are based on impulse rather than on moral judgments.

The idea of a premoral period is not new to Christian thought. For years we have talked about the age of accountability. Many Christians believe that God does not hold young children accountable for their actions. Very few would suggest that the age of accountability is reached as early as the end of Kohlberg's premoral period, around the age of five or six. We would feel more comfortable with an age of accountability that falls well into level one, or at the transition from level one to level two, after the child is well on the way to developing moral reasoning skills. But we do accept a difference in the moral responsibility of a young child and an adult.

Level One

The child who uses level one reasoning will define wrong as "those things that I am punished for." When the parent or teacher punishes, it is because the child has done wrong. But right and wrong are understood only in terms of the child's own experience. The child realizes a certain behavior, such as biting younger siblings, results in punishment, but he or she does not understand why some behaviors are wrong. When punished for biting, the child simply decides biting siblings must be wrong. To the amazement of adults, children do not generalize this discovery and conclude that hurting younger siblings in any way is wrong. Level one children apply specific rules to specific situations. One by one, the child will have to discover that hitting, pinching, and teasing others are all wrong.

At the beginning of level one the child thinks that right is obeying the commands of authorities such as parents or teachers. Within level one reasoning is developing. Gradually children come to believe that right is whatever works out for their advantage.

Early in level one the child defines justice as anything that an adult commands. Adult judgments are not questioned. Even when the child disobeys the adult command is still seen as fair--or just. Even the punishment for disobedience is considered fair.

But the concept of justice develops during level one. It comes to be defined as equality of treatment. Children are unaware of the many differences in abilities and situations they will later consider when judging what is just. Not wanting others to get ahead in any way, they value equality.

In our introductory overview of the levels of development we stated that level one is the level of self-interest. The level one child is aware of no external standards for use in making moral judgments. A parent may say, "This is right, that is wrong," but the meaning the child takes from those words is, "This is how I avoid punishment, and this is what will bring punishment." The child may respond to the commands of adults, but for reasons of self-interest—to avoid punishment and gain reward. Young children do not freely choose between self-interest and concern for others as their criterion for judging right and wrong. Since they know no better basis for judging, self-interest becomes their source of authority.

Time Out!

Choose the statement which you think describes level one reasoning.

        A. Right is obeying the rules that govern society.
        B. Wrong is what I get punished for.
        C. Justice is equal consideration for all persons.

Level one reasoning defines right as what an adult commands or what works out to my advantage. Statement "A" is therefore not an example of level one thinking.

Did you mark "B"? If so, you chose the statement that does represent level one.

Statement "C" is a definition of justice which is beyond level one reasoning. When level one thinking is fully developed there is a concern for equality of treatment, but not for equal consideration. Because of individual differences equal consideration may not lead to equal treatment. To the person at level one this would seem unfair.

What do we mean when we call level one the Level of Self-interest?

A. For persons using level one reasoning the only source they know of to guide them in making moral judgments is their own self-interest.
B. The level one person chooses to act in accordance with his or her own self-interest rather than being considerate of others.
C. When the child at level one obeys a parent or teacher he or she does so for the self-centered reasons of avoiding punishment and gaining reward.

Statements "A" and "C" are correct, but "B" is not. Young children are limited in the ability to make moral judgments because they are not aware of the needs and interests of others. Development is the process of losing these limitations.

Moving On

The reasoning used at level one is concrete reasoning. By this we mean that the child-and the adults who continue in level one-can reason only about things that can be seen and handled. Kindness is understood in terms of the nice things people do for others. Love is the acts of love which can be seen. The person using higher levels of reasoning will say, "Wait a minute. Love and kindness is so much more than an act." Yes, but we must be careful not to look down on level one thinking for the child. Coming to understand the concrete evidences of love and kindness is essential preparation for being able to grasp the richer, less obvious, more abstract aspects of these concepts. A period of concrete thinking is normal. We should be concerned about it only when older teens and adults seem to be bound to the concrete.

The attention of the child using level one reasoning is focused on the physical damage of a wrong act.

According to a level one understanding, the greater the physical damage caused, the naughtier the deed. The child gives no thought to the intentions of the wrongdoer. The little girl who cuts a large hole in her dress while trying to help her mother is naughtier than the girl who cuts a little hole in her dress while playing with scissors, something she has been told not to do. Only the size of the hole is considered in level one judging.

Persons are also valued in concrete, material terms. The following dialogue demonstrates this point. "Your daddy isn't any good," teased the elderly gentleman. "Yes he *IS!*" was the child's quick response. "Well, what is he good for, then?" asked the gentleman. With only a moment's hesitation the little girl replied, "He's good for making pancakes." At level one persons are valued for the concrete things they do. God will also be understood in these terms. God is the One who helps us avoid punishment and gives us rewards, especially material rewards.

From a level one perspective, rules are viewed as commands from some higher authority which cannot be changed. Early in level one children think they obey certain rules precisely, but their understanding of those rules is so limited that application of them is very inconsistent. Children may believe that it is essential to say "Bingo" or "I pass" at just the right point in a game. By doing this they believe they are playing by the rules of the game, not realizing the other more important rules of which they remain unaware. As the understanding of rules develops to the point where children are actually guided by them, they are moving on into level two.

At birth human infants are totally egocentric. By this we mean that they cannot distinguish between themselves and the things around them. During the first year of life they discover they are one object in a world of objects. But during the premoral period, children remain egocentric in perspective. That is, they think that everyone sees things just as they do. To begin using level one reasoning children must discover that other people have points of view different from their own. Once one has discovered that there are different ways of looking at things one begins the lifelong task of developing the ability to put oneself in the shoes of an increasing number of persons to understand how they see things. At level one the child develops the ability to understand and relate to another child's perspective if he or she has actually experienced the same situation.

Why should one do what is right? Level one reasoning replies, "To avoid punishment and to gain reward." These are the factors that will stimulate persons to do right at level one.

Time Out!

Which of the following are examples of level one reasoning?

A. Love involves the will. It is more than an act-or a feeling. True love calls for a commitment of the will.

B. Child: Sally is naughtier than John.

Adult: Remember, John had been told that he must not climb on the cupboard to get a candy. Sally was hurrying into the kitchen because her mother had called her for supper.

Child: But John only broke one cup when he was getting the candy. Sally broke fifteen cups when she pushed the kitchen door into the tray of cups. Sally is naughtier than John because fifteen is more than one.

C. The man should do everything he can to save his wife's life because funerals are expensive.

Did you choose "B" and "C"? They are correct. The child in "B" sees only the physical damage done and does not realize that intention should be considered. This is characteristic of level one reasoning.

The person making the response in "C" values human life in material terms (level one). This response came up repeatedly in research conducted in a culture where elaborate funerals were an obvious part of the way of life.

Statement "A" represents reasoning that is beyond level one. The person at level one would be aware of only the concrete, observable dimensions of love.

Mark the correct statement(s).

A. Persons using level one reasoning have a good grasp of rules and use them to guide their actions.
B. The person working through level one is able to understand and relate to another person's situation only if he or she has already had the same experience.
C. Level one persons will be stimulated to do what is right because of their desire to do their duty for society.

Only "B" represents level one reasoning. Was that what you decided?

We have seen that level one persons do not have a good grasp of rules (A). Even though they think they follow the rules just as they were given by some higher authority, there are great holes in their understanding of those rules.

As we have said, statement "B" is correct. At level one persons are beginning to be able to see another's point of view, if the person is in a situation which they have experienced.

The level one person does right to avoid punishment or pain and to gain reward or pleasure, not to fulfill a duty to society (C).

Level Two

What causes human beings to develop and learn? Kohlberg and other developmental psychologists believe that one basic cause is the fact that humans are born with a need to be competent. This need for competence causes babies to begin exploring their world and make some sense out of it for themselves. They have a need to try to discover what is going on and how things work. As children develop they begin to realize that they need help in knowing how to act. Other people seem to have information they do not have about what ought to be done. Self-centered criterion for judging right and wrong is seen as inadequate. To be competent, children need the help of external standards. As this sense of need for external standards dawns the developing person moves on into level two.

The first external standards that the level two person looks to are the actions of other persons. Children or teenagers begin to model the behavior of persons who are important to them. Right is defined as the things good people do. Wrong is what bad people do.

After living by the standards of models for some time the young person begins to discover that there are certain rules which guide the actions of those models. These rules then become his or her standards for judging right and wrong. As individuals begin living by the rules, an awareness develops of the order which rules bring to life and society. People come to value that order and the rules which create it.

With level two comes an awareness of the importance of intentions when judging the wrongness of an act. As persons first begin to consider intentions they tend to overdo it. The one who had good intentions will be excused from responsibility for an act which caused great damage.

Later in level two this leniency is tempered. As young people develop in understanding laws and grows in his appreciation for the order of society, they expect more of others. Actions are still judged by a person's intentions, but the young person also expects everyone to learn about and maintain the laws of society. It is the duty of every person to maintain the order of society which comes through obeying the law.

The order created by the laws of one's particular society is highly valued by the person who views the world through level two lenses. This person has a deep concern for maintaining those laws. If the laws are changed this may disrupt the social order. At level two all laws tend to be viewed as having equal importance. Therefore any suggested change may be seen as a threat to the society.

Time Out!

Which of the following persons do you think is using level two reasoning?

A. I think that the man should steal the drug to save his wife's life. A good husband should do anything he can to save his wife.

B. The man should not steal the drug even to save his wife's life. A good citizen will not steal. If people begin deciding when they will obey the law and when they will not, society will soon be in a state of chaos.

C. The man should not steal the drug to save his wife's life. If he does the police will catch him and put him in jail.

Both "A" and "B" are examples of level two reasoning. Note that the content--the what or should--responses are in opposition to each other, but the structure or reasoning of the responses is similar. In both "A" and "B" the persons are looking to models for standards of right and wrong--good husbands and good citizens. This is characteristic of level two. In "B" we see another level two idea. Keeping the law is valued for the sake of maintaining the order of society.

Response "C" indicates level one reasoning. Note that the "should" statement--the content--is the same as "B." But the rationale given--the structure of reasoning--is different.

The person who uses level two reasoning will: -

A. Use self-interest as the standard for judging right and wrong.
B. Want to change laws to make a better society.
C. Consider the intention when judging a person's actions.

Did you choose "C"? Good.

Level one is the level of self-interest. Level two is the level of external standards. External models and rules are the authorities used at level two for judging right and wrong (A).

We have noted that level two persons are not interested in changing laws (B). They value the order that laws bring to society and do not want that order disrupted by change.

Once persons are able to use the reasoning of level two they have lost the limitation of blindness toward intentions (C). They do take intentions and individual differences into consideration when making judgments.

Moving On

We noted that from a level one perspective the most obvious and troubling outcome of wrong actions was physical damage. When one views wrong from level two, physical damage is overshadowed by the concern for damage done to relationships between persons and in groups. Interpersonal relationships and involvement in the group are highly valued at level two.

Early in level two persons are valued for the warmth and affection that they offer or because of the affection that someone has for them. This value is based on interpersonal relationships. Later in level two, as the group and society become more important, persons are valued for the contribution they can make to society.

At level two God will be valued because of his love. The picture of God as a loving Father will be important to the level two understanding of him. Jesus will be a key model for the level two Christian. As persons develop their appreciation for law and the order it brings they will grow in their excitement over the order created by God's laws.

It is the desire to please important persons and groups that stimulates persons at level two to right actions. They do not act to avoid punishment or gain some material reward; they are more concerned about pleasing their models and doing their best for their group or society. To know they have disappointed an important person or failed in their duty to society will be more painful than physical punishment.

While young people work through level two they will be developing the ability to see things from the perspective of an ever increasing number of persons. Their ability to understand the feelings of others will be growing. At first they will comprehend the viewpoint and feelings of close friends and family. Through experiences with a widening circle of acquaintances they gradually come to understand the perspective of their own society. An understanding of how persons in other societies view the world is beyond level two.

We have seen that at level two we become aware of intentions and develop in our ability to understand the perspective of a growing number of persons. These developments lead one to be uncomfortable with a definition of justice as equal treatment for all. To decide what is just or fair individual differences and intentions must be considered. The level two person turns to the laws of society for help in knowing what is just.

Time Out!

Level two reasoning places high priority on:

A. Physical and material rewards or costs.
B. Interpersonal and group relationships.
C. The application of moral principles.

The concern of "A" represents level one reasoning. Applying moral principles will become important at level three (C).

The right completion for the above statement is "B." The concern for interpersonal and group relationships appeared several times in our discussion of level two. We saw that the damage done to relationships was what troubled persons at level two. They value persons because of their relationships, and it is the value they place on relationships with important persons and groups that causes the level two person to want to do what is right.

Which comments might be made by a person who is working through level two?

A. I'm trying to figure out what it would be like to be mom. I don't think it would be much fun to have to get supper every night of the week, especially when kids complain about the food.
B. If you are going to be just you have to treat everyone exactly the same.
C. Justice isn't as simple as treating everyone exactly the same. People have different abilities and intentions. Those differences have to be considered to know what is fair.

Did you mark "B"? I hope not, because it is a statement of a level one view of justice.

The level two view of justice can be seen in "C." Persons at level two have become uncomfortable with justice as equality of treatment. They are in a period when they are working out a more adequate understanding of justice.

In statement "A" we have a young person trying to understand the perspective of his or her mother. This could be a level two task-coming to comprehend the perspectives of persons different from themselves but still within their own circle of acquaintances or society.

Level Three

According to the moral reasoning of level three, right is the living out of moral principles which bring about justice. Wrong is anything that violates moral principles, and is unjust. As persons value laws and live by them-level two-they gain a deepening understanding of laws. Those who continue to develop begin to see that there are principles behind the laws. As they make this discovery they move on to level three. Actually, all just laws are specific applications of a few moral principles. Jesus tried to help the Pharisees see this. When they asked, "What is the greatest commandment?" Jesus replied, "'You must love the Lord your God with all your heart, and with all your soul, and with all your mind.' This is the greatest and most important commandment. The second most important commandment is like it: 'You must love your neighbor as yourself.' The whole law of Moses and the teachings of the prophets depend on these two commandments" (Matthew 22:37-40, TEV). Jesus had summed up the entire law in two principles--love God, and love your neighbor.

As people gain an understanding of moral principles and accept them as guidelines for living, they make those principles their own. Through experiences with the law and struggles to apply it in complex situations the principles behind the law are discovered, become a part of the person, and begin to control from within. At level three, external standards are less important than the moral principles persons have chosen to make their own. These internal principles are the source of authority for judging right and wrong.

But the internal principles of level three are not individualistic ideas drawn out of the air. The understanding of the principles has grown out of experience with the external standards during level two. Most of the time level three moral judgments will lead a person to obey the law, but not merely for its own sake. As persons live by their principles they will obey most laws because those laws are specific applications of a principle. Some laws, however, may be unjust. When this is the case the level three person will work to change the law.

Sometimes we find ourselves in situations where two laws are in conflict. It is impossible to obey both. Level three moral judgment is able to handle such conflicts by turning to the moral principles behind the laws. On the basis of the principles one decides what should be done.

On other occasions we may be faced with new situations for which we have no rules of conduct. Persons who use level three moral reasoning are best equipped to handle these situations. Moral principles can give guidance in any situation. Persons who must live in a complex, rapidly changing world need internal moral principles by which to live.

Time Out!

From the following statements choose those which represent level three reasoning.

A. Level three persons are free to ignore laws and external standards.
B. Wrong is what I am punished for.
C. Right is living out moral principles that bring about justice.
D. Wrong is violating moral principles and treating others unjustly.

Were "C" and "D" your choices? If so, you're doing fine.

How would you rephrase statement "A" to make it correct? Here is one correction: Level three moral judgments are based on internal principles which have developed from experience with external standards.

As we have seen, level three morality does not call for a wholesale disregard for the law (B).

As a person lives out their moral principles they will be keeping the laws that grow out of those principles. Actually, living by moral principles is more demanding than living by the letter of the law. Jesus tried to point this out in the Sermon on the Mount.

Moving On

At level three developing persons continue to broaden their perspectives. Concern arises for the feelings, needs, and viewpoint of minority groups and those who are powerless. Research indicates that carrying responsibility for the well-being of one's self and others is an essential part of developing the ability to see things from a wide range of perspectives. These experiences help to make us more sensitive to others and more thoughtful of their needs.

Justice is defined at level three as equal consideration for all persons. Highly developed level three judgments will be impartial. No favoritism will be expressed toward friends or family. Level three judgments will give equal consideration to persons from minority groups and those who are powerless. Level three persons will be champions of justice for the poor and outcasts of society.

This concern for justice will color level three reasoning. When judging the results of actions and attitudes, individuals at level three will want to know about the effect of the actions on all persons-including minority groups and the underdog. They will be as concerned when these latter groups are treated unjustly as when their friends meet injustice.

At level three persons are valued just for being persons. Personal worth is not based on the material things one can do, the affection one has to offer, or the contribution one makes to society. Personal worth is based on the principle that human life--any human life--is of great value.

As we are able to value persons for themselves we can begin to love God just for being God. Our love is not grounded on God's help in avoiding punishment, the rewards he gives, or the warmth we feel in his love.

We can love God for himself when we see no rewards and have no sense of the warmth of God's presence.

What will stimulate one to right action at level three? The level three person will not be responsive to the threat of punishment or the promise of reward. He or she will not act to gain the approval of others. It will be a commitment to moral principles that will cause the person at level three to act. To be true to oneself one must not violate the moral principles that have become a part of the self.

Time Out!

Persons at level three will:

A. Understand the perspective of a wide range of persons including those from minority groups.
B. Let society determine what justice is.
C. Be more concerned about justice for friends than for exploited persons one has never met.

"A" is the only correct statement in the above list.

Level three moral reasoning defines justice as equal consideration for all. When society does not provide this kind of equality, the level three person will challenge society (B).

One characteristic of level three judgments is a concern for those who are exploited and powerless. Statement "C" is therefore incorrect.

Which of the following are characteristics of the level three perspective?

A. Assessing the worth of a person by looking at his or her contribution to society.
B. Commitment to moral principles stimulates right actions.
C. Both of the above.

Statement "A" is characteristic of level two. At level three human life is considered sacred and all persons are valued because they are persons.

Did you choose statement "B" as correct? It is characteristic of level three.

WRAP-UP

The development of moral reasoning is a lifelong process. Each person follows a common pattern through the levels of development. Within each of the three levels there Is a great deal of development that takes place. Persons seem to move along within levels without much trouble. But making the step from one level to the next seems to present more of a challenge. A few adults never move beyond level one. Research indicates that the majority of adults use level two moral reasoning and never develop the ability to make level three judgments.

Moving from one level to the next is not something that happens overnight. Development is gradual. The person who uses level one reasoning begins to see inadequacies in his or her reasoning and makes a level two judgment now and then. Gradually this increases until most judgments reflect level two quality. Then we say this individual is operating at level two.

When people move into a new moral judgment level, they do not discard the understandings and thinking skills of the previous level. The person who can use the abstract mathematical skills of algebra may sometimes count on his or her fingers to decide the date of next Monday-a very concrete way to figure it out. The little girl who said her daddy was good for making pancakes continued to appreciate his pancake-making skills. But her appreciation for him grew as she discovered that he was a considerate husband who made a meal of pancakes for the children to let his wife enjoy a day out. The level three person values the order which law brings to society, but also sees the need to challenge unjust laws. The understandings and reasoning processes of one level are refined, expanded, and reorganized into new relationships at the next higher level.

Since the human being is a dynamic unit there will be a relationship between natural physical, mental, and moral development. Because of this, the age of children or young people gives us a clue as to the level of mental or moral development that they are likely to have reached. Children do not begin to use level one reasoning until five or six years of age. They may be as old as seven or eight when they begin.

Level one and the beginning of level two are normally the levels of childhood. It is usually between the ages of ten and twelve that children move from level one to level two. Most teenagers will use level two moral reasoning. Level three judgments should not be expected before the early or mid-twenties.

You will notice that we suggested age as a guideline for judging where children and youth are likely to be in their moral development. Age does not give us a clue for adults. Adults have the potential for level two and level three reasoning. But moral development can be inhibited and persons may be hung up at level one or two.

Reaching a certain age is no guarantee that one has reached a certain level of moral development.

Time Out!

Mark the correct statements.

A. The most crucial moral developments take place before the age of seven.
B. To move into a new level of moral development a person must discard the moral reasoning previously used.
C. Age provides a general clue to the probable level of moral development for children and early youth, but not for adults.

Since moral development is a lifelong process "A" is wrong. One of the two major steps in moral development should take place in the mid twenties or early thirties.

"B" is also wrong. A person can use the reasoning skills of any level he or she has worked through. The skills of one level are refined to become part of the new way of reasoning.

Statement "C" is correct.

PROJECTS

1. You have been reading about moral reasoning; now it is time to listen to some moral judgments. Talk with three children: a four- or five-year-old, a six- or seven-year-old, and one who is ten or eleven. Each child should be interviewed individually. Tell them the following stories. Then ask, "Which

child was naughtier? Why?" Remember, the answer to the "why" question will give you a clue to the child's moral reasoning. Probe a little on the "why."

Story I

Tommy (or Susan) was playing in the family room when his mother called him for supper. He knew mother was in a hurry to get supper over with because she was having guests later in the evening. So Tommy came running quickly. He pushed open the kitchen door with all his might. Behind the door there was a tray with fifteen cups and saucers on it. The door hit the tray, knocked the cups and saucers on the floor, and all fifteen of them broke.

Story II

There was a box of chocolates high up in the cupboard. Mother had told Mary (or Ted) that she was not to have any of the chocolates. When Mary got home from school, mother was out so Mary decided to get one of the chocolates. She climbed up on the cupboard and reached for the chocolate box. As she reached into the cupboard she knocked one cup off the shelf. It fell on the floor and broke[3]

---

[3] These stories are similar to those used by Jean Piaget in his study of the moral judgments of children. He reports his study in *The Moral Judgment of the Child* (New York: The Free Press, 1965).

2. (a) Read Matthew 5:48—6:6, 16–18.

(b) In Matthew 5:48, Jesus summarizes the standard of the Christian life. What is it?

(c) In the verses that follow this demanding standard Jesus talks about moral acts. But that is not all. He also discusses the reasons for performing those acts. In the space below list the moral acts and also the moral reasons.

	Moral Acts		*Moral Reasons*
6:2	_____	v. 2	_____
6:5	_____	v. 5	_____
6:16	_____	v. 16	_____

(d) Which is Jesus condemning, the acts or the reasons?

(e) Using the terminology introduced early in this chapter, what one word could be used to refer to the items listed under "moral acts"?_____

What word could be used for the phrases in the "moral reasons" list?

_____

(f) Read Matthew 5:17–48.

(g) What did Jesus say about his attitude toward the law? (v. 17)

46

(h) In these verses Jesus presents sets of contrasting statements. List these sets of statements.

"You have heard"	"But I say"
v. 21	vv. 22–26
v. 27	vv. 28–30
v. 31	v. 32
v. 33	vv. 34–37
v. 38	vv. 39–42
v. 43	vv. 44–48

(i) Read Matthew 7:12 and 22:36–40.
In both of these passages Jesus intimates that He has summed up the law and the prophets. Briefly state the principles which Jesus claims include the whole law.

(j) Look again at the lists from Matthew 5.
Where do you think Jesus got his "But I say" statements on God-pleasing conduct?—from the "You have heard" statements of the law, or from the principles behind the laws?

(k) Which is more demanding, to live by the letter of the law or by the principle of the law?

(adapted from Bible studies prepared by Don and Ruth Fraser, Ottawa, Ontario, Canada)

Source of Authority	Level I Self-interest	Level II External standards —models and rules	Level III Internal principles
Definitions	Right is what adults command or what brings reward. Wrong is what I am punished for—what brings pain.	Right is what good people do or what the law says one should do. Wrong is what good people do not do or what the law says one should not do.	Right is living our moral principles and being just. Wrong is violating a moral principle and being unjust.
Intentions	Oblivious to intentions.	Make allowances for intentions. Lenience tempered by sense of duty.	Consider intentions but also concerned about justice.
Justice	What adults command. Later, equal treatment.	Defined by society.	Equal consideration for all.
Value of Persons	Valued in material terms. "Persons are valuable for what they do for *me.*"	Valued because of relationships of affection and for their contribution to society.	Valued because they are persons. Human life is sacred.
Stimulus to Right Actions	Fear of punishment and desire for reward.	Desire to please important persons and perform one's duty to society.	To be true to oneself one must act upon the moral principles to which one is committed.
Ability to Take Another's Perspective	Understands the perspective of persons in situations which he has experienced	Understands the perspective of friends, family, and eventually society.	Understands the perspective of a wide range of persons including minority groups.

2.

DEVELOPMENT -- WHAT IS IT?

In chapter one we traced the path a person follows in moral development. But, someone may ask, "How does this happen?" "What is going on inside the person?" "Why does he or she see things so differently at the various levels?" Very important questions.

"Just a minute now," someone else may be saying. "Those may be important questions. But they sound pretty deep to me. Remember, I'm not a professional educator." Also an important point. Let's see how well we can do at answering the questions that have been raised, while remembering that many of you are not professional educators. We who are involved in the lives of children, youth, and adults in the church can better serve them if we have an ever deepening understanding of the inner working of our students.

Moral judgment and the living of the Christian life are influenced greatly by learning and the development of the thinking processes. As Christian educators it is important that we have an understanding of how the human mind works. How do our students learn? What is necessary for learning and development to take place? What is the pattern mental development follows? So what? These are questions that we will discuss in the following pages.

HOW DO STUDENTS LEARN?

Many answers have been given to this question. Some people teach as though they think their job is to fill an empty box with knowledge. It is as if the child's head is the empty box and the ears are funnels into that box. The teacher faithfully tells the children what they should know. As the words go through the ears into the mind the teacher assumes that the child--or adult--is learning. In this approach development toward maturity would be seen as the process of adding more and more information to the box. Maturity is reached when a certain amount of information has been taken in.

The mind is not an empty box to be filled with words. It is very active. Constantly it works with incoming sights and sounds, interpreting and organizing them. From what is heard, seen, and felt, the mind constructs a personal view of the world and what the person believes to be true.

As young children become aware of the world around them, they begin to organize things into categories. Timmy sees a brown, furry, four-legged creature and daddy says, "dog." Later a white, furry, four-legged creature runs across the yard. Mother sees it and says to Timmy, "dog." Soon Timmy begins to say "dog" when the furry four-legged animals go by. He hears them bark and pets them. These sounds and feelings are added to the sights in his mental category for "dog." He has constructed an idea of what he believes a dog is.

Then Timmy and his parents are driving in the country and he sees a monstrous furry four-legged creature. In great excitement Timmy shouts, "dog, dog,"

To his amazement daddy says, "No, son, that is a horse." Timmy must now adjust his thinking to cope with this information. This simple illustration can help us understand how learning and development take place. Let's look at it further.

We saw that Timmy had set up a category in his mind for dog. For some time he took new pieces of information in without having to make any major changes in the category. The new information just added nicely to his understanding of dogs-they come in different colors, they bark, they feel soft and warm.

But then Timmy saw the horse. He had no category for horses, so he tried to fit the horse into the best category he had for such a creature, that of dog. Had the child been alone he would have put the horse in his "dog" category and gone away believing that he had seen a monstrous dog.

Many of the young child's misconceptions about religion arise in this way. Adults talk to children about things for which they have no categories. The children-do the best they can to take care of what they have heard. Often they put the unfamiliar word or idea in a category with something that sounds similar. Examples of this can be seen in the unusual words children, in all seriousness, put to some gospel songs-Gladly the cross-eyed bear, for instance.

Children are not the only ones who walk away from church with misconceptions because they have put some idea into a wrong mental category. Since the mind actively tries to organize the things that seem to be important, these errors are often made when a person is working with a set of ideas that are new. Conversation and discussion between teachers and students are musts if teachers are going to discover these errors and help students develop their thinking by constructing new mental categories for the new ideas or rearrange their categories so that the new ideas do fit. Let's go back to our story of Timmy to see how a person sets up new categories or rearranges old categories to serve better.

When Timmy's daddy told him he was wrong and that what he thought was a big dog was really an ordinary-sized horse, he was faced with a conflict. He believed that the horse was a dog. This important person, his father, was saying it was something else. Timmy had to resolve this conflict. He could ignore the information from his father-people sometimes do this. But Timmy probably began to do some reconstructing of his thinking by setting up a new mental category for horses. His experiences in the future will add to his understanding of "horse" as he has a chance to see more horses, pet them, ride them, and see them pull a wagon. New information from these new experiences will be built into the category or understanding of horse.

When Timmy is older he will do some more reconstructing of his categories for dog and horse. He will discover that both categories can be fitted into another larger category called animals. He will then be able to have dog and horse in the same category, as he did the first time he saw the horse. But this time he will be correct, because he has reconstructed the category so that both do belong.

Timmy's mind is not an empty box to be filled with pictures and words like dog and horse, salvation and love. We have seen that the mind was actively working with what Timmy experienced. He was constructing his own ideas. No one else could do this for him. As children reconstruct their understandings of the world they develop mentally and in their ability to make moral judgments and understand God.

Time Out!

Let's look back and see whether or not all these words are making sense.

52

The seventh graders were studying kindness. They had heard stories about kind acts, and had discussed situations at school in which they could show kindness. Janie had also been involved in role playing a situation in which her friend was being unkind to another child. Sunday morning she entered the classroom, all smiles. "I tried it," she announced to the teacher. "I really tried to be nice to Sue last week. I sat by her on the bus and talked to her at recess. And do you know what? She's not a stuck-up snob. And she really seemed happy that I would sit with her and talk to her. It made me feel good too."

Would you say that Janie was:

A. Adding to her understanding of (mental category for) kindness?
B. Making an error by placing something in her "kindness" category which does not belong there?
C. Making a new category for "kindness"?
D. Reconstructing a mental category so that new ideas will fit in?

Was "A" your choice? Right on! After hearing about kindness, discussing it, and acting it out, Janie was experiencing it. She discovered that being kind leads to different impressions about people, and that kindness feels good. These were all added to her mental category for kindness.

Let's try another one.
The fifth graders who had arrived early for Sunday school were doing some research to be used later in their class period. They were beginning to read Acts 9. "Hey, what's Saul doing

here in the New Testament?" asked Steve. "I thought he was in the Old Testament." "There is a Saul in the Old Testament," answered Mike. "But this is a different one. He isn't called Saul often because his name was changed to Paul." "How about that! So there are two Sauls," muttered Steve as he went back to his reading.

Would you say that Steve was:

A. Adding to his understanding of his existing category for Saul?
B. Making an error by placing something in his existing "Saul" category that does not belong there?
C. Making a new mental category for "Saul"?
D. Reconstructing a mental category so that new ideas fit.

Have you made your choice? Was it rather hard? Different responses could be true depending on how you interpret what Steve was doing. At first Steve tried to fit the new Saul into his Old Testament "Saul" category (B). But he did not feel comfortable with this. After Mike gave him the new information he did some reconstructing of his thinking. He either created a New Testament "Saul" category (C), or broadened his "Saul" category to take in both the biblical Sauls (D).

Which of the following statements would you say are true?

A. Each person constructs his or her own understanding of the world.
B. The mind is an empty box for teachers to fill with knowledge.

54

    C. The mind organizes sights,
       sounds, feelings, and ideas into
       mental categories.
    D. Children have an uncanny ability
       to fit new information into the
       right mental categories.

Did you choose "B" and "D"? I hope not, because they are wrong. Though most of us would probably agree that the mind is not an empty box to be filled (B), many times we act as if we believe this when we begin to teach. When we act as though our only responsibility is to fill the empty box with words, our students go away with many misconceptions. Why? Because their minds try very hard to categorize the new ideas, but they do not have an uncanny ability for doing this correctly (D). They need a teacher who is trying to help them construct their own understandings rather than trying to fill them with knowledge (A).

FACTORS NECESSARY FOR
LEARNING AND DEVELOPMENT

If students need teachers who are trying to assist them in developing, it is important for us to know what causes development to take place. There are four essential causes. No one factor can explain development. If any one of the factors is absent or weak, development will be distorted, slowed down, or brought to a standstill.

Heredity and maturation influence development. Heredity has an influence on the brain. It does set some limits on a person's mental capacities. But most persons have the inherited capabilities to develop the reasoning necessary for making principled moral judgments. Humans inherit a mind that is active. Because of this inherited tendency persons are actively involved in constructing their own understandings of the world. It has also been noted that the various stages of thinking and levels of moral judgments require certain degrees of mental maturity. The normal physical maturation of the brain prepares the child for advancements in the stages of reasoning. The first influence on mental and moral development, then, has to do with the physical characteristics of heredity and maturation.

The second factor at work in development is experience with the physical world. Through direct experience with objects and events, children learn the characteristics of their world. Youngsters experiment with their world and abstract broader concepts and meanings from these experiences. A child learns what a flower is by seeing flowers, feeling them, smelling them. From these experiences the child also learns that flowers are beautiful; the world is beautiful! Experiences of wonder and joy in contact with nature may later influence the child's feelings toward the Creator God.

Direct experience is essential for the learning of young children. Babies' actions are their thoughts. Until the junior years children's thoughts are made up of the recollection of the concrete things they have experienced. It is interesting to note that some adults also think only in terms of the concrete experiences they have had.

Social interaction is the third factor involved in causing mental and moral development. Young children are not aware that anyone thinks differently than they do. Through social interaction they begin to discover that others have viewpoints unlike their own. This discovery causes them to begin to question their own perspective and uncover its inadequacies. Individuals must then rearrange their thinking so that the new ideas they are bumping into will fit in. It is in social interactions that persons run into moral conflicts. It is as one struggles to resolve these moral conflicts that moral development takes place.

We have seen that heredity and maturation, experience with the physical world, and social interaction are important to mental and moral development. But in themselves they do not explain what takes place. There seems to be another factor at work.

Different researchers have noted that humans cannot live with conflict between their understanding of the world and facts about it which are being presented to them. In the face of information which conflicts with their own perceptions they must either discount the new information or change their thinking and thus restore their inner equilibrium. This continual process of changing the structure of thinking in the light of new perceptions has been called equilibration.[4] It is the motor of development. The need to restore inner equilibrium causes a person to move on to more adequate forms of reasoning or moral judgment. Without heredity and maturation, experience, and social interaction, however, one does not become aware of conflicting ways of thinking or deciding what is moral. Without this awareness development does not take place. In summary, heredity and maturation provide the potential for development. Experience and social interaction are needed to make the potential a reality. The process of equilibration is the inner motor of development.

Time Out!

Let's pause a moment and look back.

---

[4] Piaget has identified these four stages. He calls them sensorimotor, preoperational, concrete operations, and formal operations.

The young teen class listened quietly while
Martha spoke. In her hand she held a crown of
thorns. She told her classmates how she had made
the crown and how the thorns had jabbed her
hands. It was obvious that she had been deeply
affected by the experience. She told of a new
appreciation for Christ's suffering, which was the
topic of their current unit of study.

Would you say that Mark's learning and
development were the result of:

A. Heredity and maturation?
B. Direct experience?
C. Social interaction?
D. Equilibration?

Through a direct experience with a concrete
branch of thorns, Martha had gained new
knowledge and feelings. "B" is likely the correct
answer. The maturation process may also have
been at work (A) preparing her for this experience.
But the new insights might not have come without
the experience.

Henrietta Mears stepped forward to address the
large audience. Sparkling earrings dangled above
her large fur stole. Pastor Stone slouched in his
seat, disgusted. This would be a waste of his time.
No one who looked like that could have anything
of spiritual importance to say to him. In only a few
moments, however, Pastor Stone was listening
with rapt attention. He walked from that
auditorium convinced that Henrietta Mears was a
woman of God, even though she did not dress as
he had thought Christian women should.

Would you say that Pastor Stone's change of attitude was due to:

A. Heredity and maturation?
B. Direct experience?
C. Social interaction?
D. Equilibration?

Was that a hard one? The pastor was involved in an experience and other persons were present. But probably the most important factor at work here was the process of equilibration (D). Pastor Stone was faced with a conflict between how he believed "spiritual women" looked and what he was experiencing under the ministry of a woman who did not fit his picture. He had to resolve this conflict. He did so by reconstructing his mental category for "spiritual women" so that Henrietta Mears would fit in. He had changed the structure of this thinking to restore equilibrium.

The chalkboard in the eighth grade class was filled with ideas which had come in response to the question, "How might the prodigal son's father have responded to the boy when he came home?" The seventh grade teacher who had taught this class the year before looked at the list in amazement. "You don't know how many times I asked them a 'how might' or 'what if' question," he said. "And I always got a beautiful blank."

Assuming that both the seventh and eighth grade teachers are equally skilled in leading discussions with young teens, what would you say is responsible for the different responses?

A. Heredity and maturation?

B. Direct experience?
C. Social interaction?
D. Equilibration?

Did you choose "A"? Good. Probably the difference can be explained in terms of maturation. It seems that the brain must reach a certain level of maturity before it can handle abstract thinking and consider the many possible outcomes of a situation.

The teacher had divided the class into groups of two. Each pair was asked to decide what they would tell a friend about Christianity that might influence the friend to be interested in becoming a Christian. Jane and Roger were working together.

"That's easy," began Roger, "I would just tell them that everyone has sinned and that sin will be punished unless it is forgiven. If they want to have a happy life and go to heaven some day they need to ask God to forgive their sins."

"Well, I was thinking of starting in another way," replied Jane. "I think that it is the idea of a God who loves us that causes people to be interested in Christianity. If people really believe that God loves them, they will want to respond to that love."

What cause of development has a chance to work in this situation?

A. Heredity and maturation?
B. Direct experience?
C. Social interaction?
D. Equilibration?

Do you think it is "C" and "D"? Right. Through social interaction Roger is being introduced to a reason for being a Christian which is a step higher than his own reason. He may never have thought much of God's love and a person's response to that love. The new concept introduced by Jane may cause Roger to see the missing dimension in his thinking. To restore his sense of adequacy with his own understanding and restore his equilibrium he will have to do some reconstructing of his thinking. This would cause development.

THE PATTERN OF MENTAL DEVELOPMENT

We have looked at the inner processes that are at work as a person learns and develops. We have discussed the causes of development. Extensive studies of children indicate that there is a pattern in the development of thinking processes, as well as in the development of moral reasoning.

Experiments with hundreds of children in several different countries indicate that individuals go through four stages as their thinking processes develop. We will call these stages the periods of:

1. Action intelligence
2. Prelogical thinking
3. Concrete thinking
4. Abstract thinking[5]

Not only do all persons who reach the fourth stage go through all the other stages, but everyone works through the stages in the same order. This happens

---

[5] Further instruction on teacher behaviors that facilitate openness and sharing in a class are to be found in Models of Teaching by Bruse Joyce and Marsha Weil (Englewood Cliffs, New Jersey: Prentice-Hall, Inc., 1972).

because practice in each way of thinking is a necessary preparation for the next stage. When people move from one stage to the next, they do not throw away what they have learned and the mental skills they have acquired at the previous stage. Instead they reorganize, refine, and expand their thinking. They will continue to use some lower level thinking, but they can go beyond and use more advanced mental processes. We noted earlier that we sometimes count on our fingers to figure out what date next Friday will be. We should be able to do it in our heads, just using figures, shouldn't we? Long after we are able to think abstractly--think about thoughts and ideas-- we still are helped by a good concrete example.

Although persons work their way through the stages in the same order, the speed of development is different. Also the stage at which persons stop their development varies. The four causes of development which we have discussed determine how quickly a person works through the stages and how far he or she goes.

Each of the stages reflects a different way- of thinking. Some persons have thought that maturity of thought comes from collecting more and more knowledge. But as we have seen, development of thinking comes about as the mind reconstructs its way of thinking-the structure of thought. A brief description of the four stages of thinking will point out the different qualities of thought involved.

For children in the action intelligence stage, their actions are their understandings. Children from birth to one-and-one-half or two-and-one-half years of age are in this stage. They have no words--or very few--to think in. Their actions and patterns of actions are the materials with which their minds work.

From two or three years of age to seven or eight, children operate in the prelogical thinking stage. To an adult children's reasoning seems very illogical. This is because their thoughts have not as yet been organized into rules and concepts. They see events in isolation. The importance or meaning of a sequence of events is lost on them. If you ask prelogical thinking children why a certain thing happened, they will likely give the first answer that pops into their head. It may be a magical reason, or an unrelated idea suggested by some word you used in the question. The fact that there is no adult logic to their thinking does not trouble prelogical children. They do not know there is such a thing as adult logic. As a matter of fact, children do not realize that there is any way of thinking other than their own.

Children between the ages of seven or eight and eleven or twelve use concrete thinking. We also noted that some adults do not go beyond the concrete thinking stage. At this stage reasoning takes on the characteristics of adult logic. Children become aware of the sequence of events and the relationship of one event to another. They can think back over a sequence of events to discover cause and effect relationship. This kind of thinking is called reversible thinking. It is one of the main differences between the prelogic of the child and what we have called adult logic. By thinking of past experiences, children can figure out what sequence of events is likely to follow a certain action. They are able to solve problems in thought but only if the problems relate to concrete experiences of their own. Though these children have made great strides in their thinking processes, they are still bound to thinking about concrete things or experiences.

Between the ages of eleven or twelve and fifteen or sixteen, uses of abstract thinking begin to appear. Abstract thinking persons can begin to work with ideas that are not linked with concrete images or objects. They can discuss things that can be described only with words. They can think of many possible results that might come from an action, even though they may not have experienced most of the results. Many Christian concepts cannot be fully understood until a person can think abstractly.

Time Out!

Are you ready to check yourself again?

Match the stages of thinking and the descriptions which follow.

_____ a. Action intelligence

1. Reasoning is logical but people think in terms of concrete experiences

_____ b. Prelogical thinking

2. The mind has not organized thought into rules and concepts. Events are seen in isolation and the child is unaware of the significance of a sequence of events.

_____ c. Concrete thinking

3. The person can think about things which can be described only in words. He or she can think about many possibilities including some not personally experienced.

_____ d. Abstract thinking

4. Children's actions are their thoughts.

If you have a-4, b-2, c-1, and d-3, you are right.

SO WHAT?

You may be asking, "But why do I need to know that? I'm interested in the moral and spiritual development of my students, not their intellectual development." The interesting thing is that moral and spiritual development are closely related to the development of thinking and reasoning. Persons do not begin to function at moral development level one until they are leaving the prelogical thinking stage and moving into concrete thinking. To advance in level one, concrete thinking is required. Abstract thinking is necessary for level two moral development and beyond.

How would the stage of development of a person's thinking influence his or her application of the Golden Rule? We have noted that children using prelogical thinking do not see the relationships between events. They cannot step outside of themselves and ask, "How does Johnny feel when I take the truck from him?" These children are aware only of their own feelings. It is impossible for them to understand the Golden Rule. They do not comprehend the connection between their actions and another child's feelings. In a crisis moment their attention is completely focused on their own feelings.

Children--or adults--using concrete thinking are able to see the relationship between their actions and another person's feelings. They are able to think-of possible actions and their probable results. By deciding which results they would like to experience, they can decide on a course of action in line with the Golden Rule. Concrete thinking, however, limits persons to thinking about concrete actions and results which they have experienced in the past. In an unfamiliar situation they will not be able to apply the Golden Rule.

Abstract thinking allows a person to take into consideration more of the factors that may be at work. The person can be aware of feelings and possible responses that are unknown to the younger child. A deep understanding of the other person's situation is needed to be able to fully apply the Golden Rule. This requires experience and mature thinking.

People's ways of thinking also determine how they can conceive of God and their own relationship to God. Young children understand God in terms of their own experience. God is an adult who is bigger and wiser than fathers and mothers. God punishes those who are bad and loves those who are good. Concrete thinking allows children to have a clearer understanding of God. But the concept of God is limited to an understanding of his concrete acts. Only through abstract thinking can persons discover the deep purposes behind God's acts. Many of the attributes of God are beyond the understanding of those who cannot think abstractly. The concrete thinking child can know what acts result from God's love or God's holiness. But love and holiness are more than specific acts. They are big concepts. Abstract thinking is needed to explore them. As thinking processes develop an ever greater understanding of God is possible. Individuals may not choose to use their intellectual potential in knowing God. But immature thinking limits what one can understand of God.

An understanding of the stages of development in thinking can also help us communicate with our students. If we know how they think we know better how to plan their learning experiences. We have a better idea of what is within their capabilities. Different kinds of content, questions, and activities are appropriate for different stages of mental development.

In this chapter we have discussed how development takes place and the close relationship between mental development and moral and spiritual development. What does all this have to say to Christian educators? In the last two chapters we will discuss some answers to that question.

PROJECTS

1. Listen carefully to the children you meet this week. Engage them in conversation and note the different ways in which they think.

2. Here is a sample experiment you can try. On a piece of paper draw a large "3" and a "7" that is much smaller. Ask several children which number is larger. Be sure to show your numbers to a four-year-old, a six- or seven-year-old, and an older child. Do they all give the same response?

3 (a) Read Ephesians 1:17-20; 3;14-19; Colossians 1:9-12.

   (b) These are prayers Paul prayed for his friends. What are the requests he makes?

   (c) Judging from these requests, what do you think Paul's attitude would be toward mental development? Give reasons for your answer.

   (d) What other scripture portions canyou think of which emphasize the importance of the mind or knowing?

3.

THE ATMOSPHERE FOR MORAL DEVELOPMENT

For the last fifteen minutes the noise from the seventh grade classroom had been building steadily. Someone had to intervene. Before entering the room Stan glanced through the window in the door. Sally, the adult leader of the group, sat in one corner of the room apparently listening to two girls recite their memory work. The boys were chasing each other around and over the chairs, swatting at anyone who came within arms' length. "What a waste of time," muttered Stan as he opened the door. "Those boys aren't learning a thing."

Do you agree with Stan? Is time being wasted for the boys? We would probably agree with him at that point. But are the boys learning anything? Let's look at that question. Undoubtedly the boys are not learning what Stan feels they should learn through the activities of their church young teen youth group. But they are learning, for learning is a continuous process. The boys may be learning that if you want to have fun at church activities you have to make your own fun. They may be learning that their teacher does not really understand them and their needs. They may be coming to feel that she does not care about them, but they are learning. The question is, what are they learning?

We tend to think of teaching and learning only in terms of the things which teachers teach. If children learn what the teacher has tried to teach, we say that they have learned. If they did not learn what the teacher tried to teach, we say they did not learn. But the teacher is not the only source of learning. Children, and adults, for that matter, are learning from everything that is happening to them. The environment and atmosphere of the classroom are powerful teachers. Some of the most important things in life are learned from the environment in which we live, without any direct teaching. Few people would set out to teach children that they are stupid, a bother, and unimportant. But when adults insist on doing things for children, fail to praise their accomplishments, deride them for their failures, sigh when they want something, and never have time for them, children learn the lesson well. They see themselves as stupid, bothersome, and unimportant. From the unplanned curriculum of this environment, children learn a crippling self-concept.

The atmosphere or environment teaches more subtly than the planned curriculum, but the impact of the unplanned curriculum may have a deeper, more lasting influence. Those who are concerned about moral development will want to give careful attention to the unplanned curriculum-the atmosphere and environment in which the child is developing.

In the study of moral development it has been noted that the kind of environment in which children live influences their progress in development. For example, an understanding of what is fair or just will develop if a person is part of a family and a class which treats people fairly. If children do not experience justice, they may never come to fully understand what justice is.

One of the most important things an adult can do to help children develop morally is to provide them with the kind of atmosphere that facilitates moral development. Several characteristics have been identified as essential to a healthy environment of moral development. We will discuss four of these: mutual respect, a sense of belonging, justice, and openness. But first let's take a moment for review.

Time Out!

In the preceding paragraphs the phrase "unplanned curriculum" was used to refer to:

A. A poorly planned lesson.
B. Everything that happens to the student other than what the teacher had planned as a learning experience.
C. The negative things that happen in a classroom.

Was "B" your choice? Then you got the point. In our discussion we used the illustration of a poorly planned or unplanned lesson and the negative things that were learned, but positive things can also be learned from the unplanned curriculum. The environment can facilitate moral development. The unplanned curriculum will be more likely to have a positive influence if we study the environment in which our students are learning and work at making it healthier for development.

MUTUAL RESPECT

One of the signs of a healthy environment for moral development is mutual respect. Children respect the adults and other children in their world, but the adults must also communicate the fact that they respect the children, their feelings, and perspectives. In homes where parents continue to use authoritarian rule to control the family their children are stunted in their moral development. Children need the experience of being involved in the setting of rules and the decision-making of the family and the classroom. Parents have been known to say, "You do as I say and don't ask why!" Children need to ask why. They need to feel that they are important. They need to watch someone trying to see things from their point of view.

If children are to experience an atmosphere of mutual respect, adults must come to respect the child. Sometimes we seem to think of children as second class citizens just waiting to grow up and become first class citizens-adults. If we believe that the process of growth and development is part of God's creative plan, we must value children as they are. A four-year-old with prelogical thinking is doing just as God intended four-year-olds to do. He or she has just mastered the learning of a language in much less time than it takes an adult to learn a second language. The child's ability calls for our respect.

Children are born with great potential for development. We have noted that from birth they are actively involved in trying to make sense out of their world. They will develop mentally, physically, and morally, unless that development is thwarted. Adults often become so wrapped up in what they are trying to do to help a child learn that they lose sight of what the child is doing. A greater respect for, and trust in the child's capabilities and accomplishments would make us better facilitators of moral development.

The way children view the world is an important part of their process of development. They must come to fully understand their world in concrete terms before they are ready to explore the abstract ideas that are behind the concrete events. A child may say, "Love is doing nice things for people." The adult might answer, "But there is more. The kind act is only an expression of love. Love is an attitude, a response to others, a set of the will." An understanding of the acts of love and their results, however, is an essential step in the process of coming to understand love in its fuller dimensions. Every level of development is important. It is necessary for children to master the skills of thinking, feeling, and doing at one level to prepare them for entering into the next level of development. The concepts of prelogical children or their sibling who uses concrete thinking are to be valued. Even when we as adults can see the inadequacies of the child's concept we should respect it as an important expression of a developing mind and growing person.

Out of respect for children, adults should try to see things from their point of view. One of the main reasons for studying children's thinking and moral reasoning is so that we can better understand their perspective. When we know the path they follow in development, we understand why children see things as they do. We are aware of the importance of each phase of development and respect children and their abilities.

Time Out!

Which of the following statements describe an important characteristic of a healthy atmosphere for moral development?

A. Children respect the authority of adults.
B. Adults respect the rights of children.
C. Adults respect the abilities, feelings, and rights of children and the children respect each other and adults.

"C" describes the situation which we have called mutual respect. A growing consideration and respect for others is an important part of moral development. It is therefore important for children to respect adults and other children, but that respect and consideration must be first demonstrated by the adult if development is to be facilitated.

When we stop to consider the great accomplishments of children and realize that development is a natural process taking place within the child, which of the following responses would you say is most appropriate?

A. Adults should acknowledge that all they need to do is give the child freedom to develop.
B. Adults should respect the capabilities of children and try to find ways to work with them as both children and adults continue to develop together.
C. Though children do make great strides intellectually, in comparison to adults they are still very limited and need adults to set rules and direct them.

Respect for the child's capabilities does not result in a "hands off" policy on the part of the adult (A). Children will profit from adults who are interested in their development and work with them (B), but when adults look down on children and are afraid to trust their abilities those adults retard the development of the children in their care (C).

Sandy has just given her definition of love, "Love is doing nice things for people." Which teacher response(s) do you think shows respect for the child?

A. "That is an important part of love. We do show our love by the things we do, but let's look at 'nice actions.' Is love the only reason for doing nice things for others?"

B. "No, love is not the things we do. Love is what causes us to do what is nice."

C. "That's a good answer, Sandy. We do show our love through the nice things we do for others."

Did you choose "A" and "C"? Both of these responses show respect for the child's thinking. The teacher giving response "A" demonstrates respect for the child's present concept of love but goes on to open a new window for the child. By leading the children to consider the reasons behind actions the teacher is opening the way for them to discover new aspects of the concept of love. Teacher "A" is trying to work with the child in the process of development.

Moving On

Mutual respect, then, requires that adults honestly respect children. Another factor that influences the atmosphere of mutual respect is the teacher's view of his or her role.

Often we tend to think of the teacher as the one who knows and the student as the one who is to learn. The teacher is the one who has the facts or truths that are to be transmitted to the learners. Many times the methods we use indicate that we think teachers can transplant full-grown concepts into the minds of learners as they passively listen to the teacher. This view of the teacher's role destroys mutual respect and inhibits development.

Mutual respect calls for teachers who see themselves as learners. Development and learning should be lifelong processes. As we assist children in the exploration of concepts and in expanding their reasoning processes we too can be learning. We may learn, not only with the children, but from the children. A teacher who expects this will create an atmosphere of mutual respect.

We noted earlier that knowledge and moral reasoning cannot be transmitted or transplanted from the mind of one person directly to the mind of another. Each person must construct his or her own understandings and develop his or her own reasoning processes. What, then, should be the role of the teacher?

Teachers who are concerned about moral development should see their role as that of facilitators of development. We cannot make other people learn or develop. We cannot *give* them concepts or values, but we can help or facilitate them as they learn and develop. The facilitator role for teachers is a mutual respect role. Teachers have an important helping role to play but acknowledge that the child has an equally important role to play in the learning process.

When we see ourselves as facilitators our attention is focused on learners' needs and interests. If we are to help students learn, nothing we do has meaning apart from their needs and progress. Our goal is to work with our students, knowing them, listening, and responding to them.

Sometimes the facilitator may introduce students to new ideas. In our last illustration teacher "A" was endeavoring to introduce students to new ideas about love through the use of questions. In response to the questions the students will take another look at their actions and the reasons for them. As they explore intentions they will have opportunity to discover new aspects of love. Teachers may introduce their students to new ideas through field trips, films, meeting new people, debates, discussions, stories, lectures--the list could go on and on. The teacher may introduce the new idea, but the students work with that new idea, explore it, interpret it, and fit it into their thinking. The learners construct their concepts, the teacher facilitates the process.

At other times the facilitator acts as counselor, consultant, friendly critic. Students may ask for advice or information. They may share questions that are troubling them. Rather than giving direct advice the teachers will be of more assistance to students if they help the students think things through and discover the answers for themselves. Sometimes the actions of children or young people are hurting either themselves or others. When this is the case the teacher or parent may need to take the role of friendly critic. Here again the adult will be of most help to young people by helping them think through what is happening and by leading them in exploring better ways of acting.

The facilitator may also act as a sounding board or reflector. Students may be helped to see their attitudes, emotions, or ideas more clearly as a parent or teacher restates them and reflects them back to the learner. In this role the adult is working through the process of learning with the student. Together they are looking for the problem or inadequacies and searching for better ways of understanding and acting.

To act effectively as facilitator of learning the teacher must earn the respect of the student. Young people will not come to us for counsel unless they respect us and are convinced that we care about them. Without respect "friendly" criticism is resented and efforts to help clarify the problem by reflecting attitudes and emotions will be ignored. We earn respect through respect. When we respect children and take a genuine interest in them, they will respond with respect. To be worthy of respect we must also be authentic. To expect one thing of the child and do another ourselves is to destroy respect. If we preach one standard and live by another we should not expect respect.

Time Out!

Which of the following statements would be made by teachers likely to develop an atmosphere of mutual respect in the classroom?

A. There is one problem with teaching the second grade Sunday school class. I never get a chance to attend an adult class where I can learn some new things myself.
B. Many times when I'm preparing to teach my first graders I discover exciting new insights in the Scriptures. The faith of those six-year-olds is often a challenge to me.
C. Some of the most profitable discussions with my young teens have come after I have admitted that I don't know the answer to a question. When we all become searchers--teacher and students--exciting things happen.

Teachers "B" and "C" see themselves as learners. They will be more likely to foster mutual respect with their students than teacher "A" who does not seem to be a learner on Sunday mornings.

Teachers concerned about moral development should take the role of facilitator because:

A. No one can give another person knowledge or wisdom. We can only help others construct their own understandings.
B. Persons are actively involved in the business of learning. What they need is someone alongside guiding them and helping to make their efforts at learning as productive as possible.

C. Children ignore what they are told. They respond only when adults help them make their own discoveries.

Did you choose "A" and "B"? These are two important reasons for assuming the role of facilitator. Although "C" is not correct as it is stated, it does suggest another reason for acting as a facilitator. Sometimes teenagers and adults do ignore what they are told. Often people do not understand what they are told. Persons of all ages are more likely to act on discoveries that they have been helped to make for themselves than on instructions they have been given.

A facilitator may act as:

A. Introducer of new ideas
B. Counselor
C. Consultant
D. Friendly critic
E. Reflector or sounding board

Did you mark all of the items above? Good. These are all activities of the facilitator which we have discussed.

Which of the following conditions must exist before one can act as a facilitator?

A. The teacher must establish discipline in the class.
B. The teacher must come to believe that the content of learning is not important.
C. The teacher must earn the respect of the students.

"C" is the desired answer. Was that your choice? The earned respect of the students is a prerequisite for facilitating moral development.

A SENSE OF BELONGING

Mutual respect involves not only teacher-student relationships but also student-student relationships. The sense of community and togetherness in a group affects the influence that group will have on those who are a part of it. If students are going to be free to share their concerns and be honest about what they think and how they feel, they must feel safe and accepted in the group.

Establishing acceptance and caring within a group is not always easy. Some children are regularly excluded by others. When teens do not know each other they do not trust. Opening up to others is often difficult for teenagers. It is much easier to enjoy their comfortable little group and let the outsiders or newcomers go their own way. But the sense of belonging within the learning group is important to development. It should be one of the teacher's major concerns.

The teacher can begin by giving students opportunities to get better acquainted with each other. Parties, all day or weekend outings provide informal settings in which teacher and students can come to know each other better. A day of hiking or an evening of fun in the teacher's home will do more to build a sense of groupness than months of weekly formal study sessions.

Help the students become aware of the special strengths of the various class members. Give students opportunity to use their abilities and share their knowledge.

Teachers can also help students think positively about differences rather than ridiculing them. When differences are discovered in a class these can be explored with interest. The students can come to understand some reasons for differences of opinion. They can look at the ways in which differences add to life. The teacher who accepts differences can help students accept those differences also.

When there is a problem in class relationships, the teacher should face it and work toward a solution. This may mean helping a child come to understand how the things he or she does bothers others. It may mean spending time with a child or young person whose bid for attention in the class is obnoxious to the other students. Exclusiveness may need to be pointed out to a group of teens and a solution sought, together. Often we tend to live with a problem and hope that it will go away, but whenever the sense of community in a group or for any person in that group is in danger the teacher should actively seek to restore it.

Time Out!

Moral development is more likely to take place in a group which has a keen sense of unity or community. The individual will be helped most by a group when he or she feels valued as a part of that group. In the last month what have you done to help build the sense of community and belonging in your class?

A. Provided informal fun times so that teacher and students could get better acquainted.
B. Took time to help a student find ways of overcoming problems that were causing exclusion from the group.
C. Enlisted the help of leaders in the class in making a newcomer or outsider feel more a part of the group.
D. Discussed with the group an action which was destroying the sense of unity in the class.

Together we searched for ways of solving the problem.

E. Listened to students tell of important events in their lives.

F. _____

Are you satisfied that you have done all that is needed to make your class a caring community? Or do you see other things that you can do?

EXPERIENCES OF JUSTICE

In chapter 1 we noted that as persons develop morally, their concept of what is just changes. An understanding of what is fair or just is an important factor in making mature moral decisions. If children are to develop in their understanding of justice, they must experience justice. Those who are concerned about moral development must give attention to the justice of the treatment they give.

Justice might be defined as equal consideration for all. How often do we as adults stop to consider what the child would want before we make a decision? Do we ask ourselves how our actions make the child or teenager feel? Usually we are more aware of the desires and feelings of outgoing children. Do we try to find out what the quiet, reserved children would want, or do they feel that no one knows or cares about them and their interest? Answering these questions will give the teachers an indication of the quality of justice that they are providing.

Time Out!

Which of the following statements would you say are important reasons for being concerned about the quality of justice in the classroom?

A. A person's understanding about justice influences his or her ability to judge what is right and wrong. Just treatment helps develop a mature understanding of justice.
B. Adults have often failed to give consideration to the interests and feelings of children and youth when making decisions.
C. It is easy to overlook quiet students and their needs.

Did you mark all three? If so, you are on target.

OPENNESS

The atmosphere that is most healthy for moral development is characterized by mutual respect, a sense of community, justice, and openness. By openness we mean the freedom to express ideas, questions, and feelings. One of the four factors necessary for moral development is social interaction. Persons need to be sharing their ideas with others and discovering how they view things. In an atmosphere of openness ideas and different perspectives flow freely. Students are learning from each other. They are bumping into new ideas and being caused to question their own thinking.

If teachers are to work with students to facilitate development, they need to know what is going on in the minds of the students. Only as persons express ideas, reasons, and feelings can we get a glimpse of the functioning of their mind. The open sharing of viewpoints is essential for the teacher who is trying to help students develop.

"Agreed," you may be saying, "but how do you get kids to open up and share what they are thinking?" This question has expressed the frustrated cry of many a teacher, but it does have some answers.

Persons will feel free to open up and share their deep thoughts, questions, and concerns only if they have a deep sense of belonging to the group.[6] If they fear rejection they will not open up, but if they believe the group will accept them no matter what they think or say they are then free to be open. We must learn to love and accept persons with whom we disagree.

The way in which the teacher and other class members respond to statements will have a lot to do with whether or not there is openness in a class. The teacher should encourage students to express all points of view. Every idea should be accepted as being worthy of examination. Note, we did not say that every idea must be accepted as right, but every idea is worthy of consideration if it is of importance to a member of the class. No idea should be put down as too ridiculous to be considered. That kind of response will quickly kill openness.

Openness is fostered when students are led to believe that they have important contributions to make to the class. They will question and probe others when they realize there are also exciting things they can learn from the group.

Finally, emphasizing the ongoing nature of learning will encourage openness and the expectation of learning together. This concept is communicated as the

---

[6] Values Clarification is explained in *Values and Teaching: Working with Values in the Classroom* by Louis E. Raths, Merrill Harmin, Sidney B. Simon (Columbus, Ohio: Charles E. Merrill, 1966).

teacher acknowledges that he or she has much to learn and is expecting to learn from students. As leaders in the group talk about answers for which they are still searching it becomes easier for everyone to openly explore their own questions.

Time Out!

We have discussed the importance of an atmosphere which encourages the free expression of ideas. Why is this important to moral development?

A. Students enjoy freely expressing their thoughts. Experiences which foster moral development should be enjoyable.

B. When ideas are freely expressed students are bumping into new ideas, they are pushed-to question their own thinking, and they learn from one another.

C. Teachers depend on the ideas their students express to know how to work with them to facilitate their development.

Although we like to make learning experiences enjoyable not all experiences leading to moral development will be fun. Sometimes moral development results from realizations that are unpleasant and call for changes that are hard. Statement "A," therefore, is not correct. Were "B" and "C" your choices? If so, good, because they state two of the main reasons for fostering an atmosphere of openness in the classroom.

Judging from their comments, which of the following teachers do you think is fostering an atmosphere of openness?

A. "Sam has raised a good question. He says that he just can't buy the picture of God which appears in Joshua and Judges. How do some of the rest of you deal with this issue?"

B. "We have a good list of ideas here, but before we begin to discuss them, can you think of any other concepts of what God is like?"

C. "I like that idea. I'd never thought of it that way before. I'm learning something new every day."

D. "Pam, you should never question what God does. His ways are higher than our ways and we must never forget that."

Did you choose "D"? I hope not. In the future Pam and the rest of the class will keep their questions and doubts to themselves. Who wants to get pounced on in public? The students have learned that the safe thing to do is to give the teacher the answer that is wanted. The teacher is now cut off from the information he or she needs to facilitate development. When students close in their thoughts there is no way of knowing where they are in their development and what their needs are. Teacher "A" is fostering an atmosphere of openness by accepting Sam's comment as worthy of consideration. Teacher "B" is encouraging the students to express many points of view. The ongoingness of learning is being demonstrated by teacher "C." All of these teacher behaviors foster an atmosphere of openness in the classroom.

Moving On

Quietly but powerfully the atmosphere in which our students live is teaching. The question that cries out for an answer from concerned teachers is, "What are my students learning from the environment that I create for them?"

PROJECTS

1. In the light of the ideas in this chapter, how do you feel about the atmosphere or environment of your class (or home)? Are you satisfied? Is it healthy, or is there room for improvement?

   Think of the four components of an environment healthy for moral development. Is there something that you can do to improve:
     -mutual respect
     -sense of belonging
     -experiences of justice
     -openness?

   Choose the component that you think most needs improvement.

   Plan to do at least one thing to improve the atmosphere in your class or home. Do it this week.

   I plan to:

When?

2. (a) Read Ephesians 4. Make note of any concepts in Ephesians 4 which relate to the ideas discussed in this chapter.

(b) Look more closely at verses 1-6, 11-16, 25-32.

What do these verses have to say that would help to foster mutual respect, a sense of belonging, justice, openness?

	Mutual Respect	Sense of Belonging	Justice	Openness
1-6				
11-16				
25-32				

4.

IS THERE MORE?

From what we have said in chapter three, it would seem that the teacher is to respect the students, help them respect each other, treat them fairly, and let them speak their minds. Is that it? Or is there more that we can do to help others develop morally? The kind of learning community which we create is important, but that is not all there is to facilitating moral development. In this final chapter we want to explore further the teacher activities which are important to moral development.

In chapter 2 we discussed the four causes of development. Two of these causes--heredity/maturation and the process of equilibration--take place inside the learner and are not in the control of the teacher or parent. The other two factors--direct experience and social interaction--have to do with the environment of the learner. The adult can and does influence these factors profoundly.

Parents and teachers can do much to provide children and youth with the kinds of experiences which will help them develop. Under the label of experiences we will look at both (1) direct experiences with the physical world and events and (2) experiences of social interaction.

From experiences of life each person constructs his or her understandings of the world. The richer the experiences the more one has to work with for building broad comprehensive concepts and perspectives. We will want to provide a wide range of experiences for our students, but what kinds of experience will be important?

PROVIDE EXPERIENCE:

To Develop Thinking Skills

We have noted that moral development is related to the development of thinking abilities. A person who thinks deeply and maturely in some areas may not develop in moral reasoning. However, a person who has not developed his or her reasoning abilities cannot make mature moral judgments. Reasoning abilities are the tools used in making moral judgments. Any experiences which help the child, youth, or adult develop intellectually are assisting moral development. Giving preschool children opportunities to explore the physical world with their eyes, ears, and hands, providing items for them to sort into categories or giving them pictures to arrange in proper sequence may seem to be far removed from moral development. These activities help children develop mentally and prepare them for using those thinking skills in the area of moral judgments.

To Exercise Moral Reasoning

Once a new ability is gained, a person wants to use or exercise it. Exercise is important preparation for acquiring additional skills. This is true of moral reasoning. Children, youth, and adults need to exercise their moral reasoning and master the level they have attained so that they can then go on to more mature judging. The discussion of moral dilemmas can provide moral reasoning exercises. The teacher or parent tells a story of a child faced with a difficult moral decision. At the close of the story the listening child is asked what the child in the story should do and why. In these kinds of discussions adults are often satisfied when the child gives the "right" answer to the "should" question. But the "why" question is extremely important. Through exploring the "why" the child exercises moral reasoning. Moral dilemma discussions can take place as a family rides in the car together, as parents and children work together, or as they chat together at bedtime. Curriculum materials for Christian education programs often suggest the use of moral dilemma discussions. The dilemma must suggest genuine conflict that the child or young person can comprehend.

Even better than discussing fictional situations is the discussion of dilemmas that the child or teenager actually faces. If a ninth grader happens to mention being troubled by a friend who keeps asking to copy his or her homework, the teacher or parent of the teen quickly gives advice and hurries on. At another time the same adult, using a fictional account, may try to lead the teen in exploring what ought to be considered when deciding whether or not to share homework and why certain actions are desirable or undesirable. How much more profitable the discussion would have been if it had taken place in the real situation when the teenager needed to think the issue through. Adults tend to be so busy and wrapped up in their own world that they don't notice the opportunities or take the time to help the child or teen exercise moral reasoning skills when it would count most, in the real moral dilemmas of life.

To Give Meaning

For Julie "dog" means a soft, warm, friendly four-legged animal. For Kevin "dog" means a loud, frightening four-legged animal. What makes the difference? Their experiences with dogs. Words such as love, justice, and worth of persons are important in moral reasoning. Their meanings will grow out of experiences. These experiences will influence moral development. As the first grade teacher takes time to listen to Steve tell about his new guppies, Steve is learning that he is important—a person of worth. When he waits his turn as Karen tells what her kitten did he is learning that Karen too is a person of worth. In the family or classroom where children are asked for their opinions or viewpoints and their ideas are taken seriously, those children are experiencing consideration and learning the meaning of justice. Through experiencing genuine forgiveness children or teens learn an important facet of the meaning of love. Adults concerned about moral development will want to provide experiences that give meaning to love, justice, and the worth of persons.

Time Out!

From the list of factors causing moral development—heredity/maturation, experience, social interaction, and equilibration—we have suggested that parents and teachers give special attention to experience and social interaction. What would you say is the reason for this emphasis?

A. In the final analysis, influences in the environment are what shape a person's development.

B. All four factors of development are important but adults can most readily influence experience and social interaction.

C. Both of the above.

Did you choose "B"? Good. Probably the word "shape" gave you the clue that reason "A" was not the desired response. Remember, persons are not shaped. Each individual constructs understanding from his or her own experiences and social interactions. The environment has an important influence on development, but the inner processes of the individual must not be overlooked. They too make a big difference.

Which of the following teachers do you think is likely to be most successful as a facilitator of moral development?

A. "That's right, David, Vickie should not cheat on her spelling test. Now I'm going to read you another story. This one is about Jeff. When I finish I want you to tell me what Jeff should do."

B. "And so, Vickie learned that it is wrong to cheat. She discovered that when she cheated she hurt herself. Cheating keeps us from becoming the best persons we can be."

C. "Several of you seem to agree that Vickie should not cheat. Why do you think that it is wrong for her to cheat?"

Each of the teacher quotes imply that the class is looking at a story presenting a moral dilemma. Teacher "B" seems to be telling the students what should be done and why without giving them opportunity to exercise their moral reasoning skills. Teacher "A" is asking the students what should be done in the situation. They are using some thinking skills, but did you notice that the teacher did not introduce the important "why" question? Teacher "C" is probably doing most to facilitate moral development because both the "should" and the "why" questions are introduced. Teacher "C" is providing opportunity for the students to exercise their moral reasoning skills by exploring the reason--the why--behind a moral action.

Mr. Snell is trying to help his class of eighth graders grow in their understanding of the feelings of others. He wants them to discover why it is important to be considerate of others when they make choices. Which of the following approaches will be likely to be most effective?

A. The eighth graders wandered into the room looking like six storm clouds. Obviously they were displeased with something. After a little probing Mr. Snell discovered that they were angry with the ninth graders who were planning a trip to the sand dunes and didn't want any "little eighth graders" along. "Just by looking at you I know you don't like what's happening," commented Mr. Snell. "But can you describe to me how you feel?" The discussion led into why they felt as they did and how others feel when they are left out.

B. Mr. Snell knew that going bowling and then having a pizza together was one of the favorite activities for his eighth graders. To start the class session on Sunday he would tell of an unpopular young teen who discovered that his class was having a bowling and pizza party but he was not invited. By asking how the boy would feel and why, Mr. Snell planned to lead the class into a discussion of being considerate of others.

C. Mr. Snell was preparing to lead his class in a discussion of the need for considering others when making decisions. He remembered an article he had just read about striking auto workers. They were striking because they did not feel that they were being treated as human beings. That would be just the article to use as a starter for class discussion.

Each of the three approaches presents a dilemma for discussion. Each discussion would provide some exercise in moral reasoning, but which approach would be best? "A"? Right. Real dilemmas usually provide the best opportunities for new understandings. Approach "B" would be next best. It is preferred over "C" because it is closer to the experiences of the teens.

Experiencing love, justice, and the worth of persons is important to moral development because:

A. These experiences will be rewarding and cause the child or teen to act morally.

B. These experiences will be enjoyable and students develop most when they are enjoying themselves.

C. The meanings of words and concepts grow out of experiences.

"C" is the best answer. How did you do? Moral actions based on a reward system is inadequate (A). What happens when rewards are not being handed out? Answer "B" is also unacceptable. Later in the chapter we will see that often difficult, unsettling experiences are very effective stimulators of moral development.

Moving On

To Broaden Perspective

Mature moral judgment rests heavily on the ability to see things from the perspective of other persons. Moral development will be enhanced through experiences that broaden a person's perspective--introduce him or her to other viewpoints. It is through the social interaction of play and childish squabbles that children first discover that not everyone sees things just as they do. All through life, experiences of social interaction help to broaden our perspectives. As our circle of acquaintances grows, as we see how others live, and learn what they think, we know better how to treat them justly. Through these experiences we learn new things that need to be considered when deciding what ought to be done in a given situation. Not until we understand how other persons think and feel can we put ourselves in their shoes and decide how to act out the Golden Rule.

Parents and teachers can provide opportunities for social interaction which will introduce learners to other perspectives. A class is often made up of students with very different backgrounds. Teachers should encourage students to get acquainted, share their ideas and feelings. Where students are all quite similar it would be helpful if the teacher planned to let them get to know children their age from a different type of community, race, or socioeconomic group. Getting together once to look at one another awkwardly will not do the trick, but when an African-American child and a white child, a child from the city and one from the country have a chance to become friends, they all profit.

Experiences with persons of different generations will also help to broaden perspectives. Grandparents assisting in the preschool department or a party for senior citizens put on by teenagers would provide good experiences. A junior class might adopt a grandmother. They could do special things for her, visit with her, and get to know her. Families who are separated from grandparents, aunts, and uncles could adopt substitutes from the church family. Many of these suggestions may seem to be far removed from the important business of moral development. Let's remember, children who have a wide range of social interactions seem to develop more rapidly in moral reasoning than those with fewer social interactions.

Through the social interaction of the class or family persons are introduced to moral reasoning which is more mature than their own. As Tom describes why he thinks children should not lie, Sue hears reasons that she had never thought of before. She discovers inadequacies in her own reasoning. The new rationale is attractive to her so Sue adjusts her thinking to take in the new ideas.

In his research Kohlberg has noted that persons cannot understand moral reasoning that is more than one step above the moral judgments of which they are capable. After learning this, some teachers and parents have set out to discover the level of moral development at which their children are functioning. Then they try to match what they say to the child's thinking by speaking to them from one step above. This is probably not necessary. Children, teenagers, or adults who live in an environment rich in social interaction will naturally bump into reasoning which is just beyond them.

Kohlberg also finds that persons are attracted to reasoning that is just beyond them, rather than to lower levels of thinking. Children who bump into new reasons for being truthful or new ideas about fairness that are just beyond their present thinking will be attracted to these. As they adjust their thinking to take in the new, they will be developing. The concern of the teacher or parent, therefore, should be to provide an environment rich in opportunities for discussions and the sharing of ideas. This social interaction may be during organized times when the group is working together or it may take place informally as students have the chance to talk about the things that are of special importance to them.

A person's understanding of how another feels and thinks is increased through role-taking experiences. Role-taking means actually performing a certain role and accepting the responsibilities of that role. The importance of role-taking is wrapped up in the fact that meanings grow out of experiences. For example, the value of dependability will not be fully comprehended -by teenagers until they have been in a position of dependence on others.

Tom, Karen, Doug, and Linda were preparing a musical presentation for a program the teens were putting on for their parents. Tom, Karen, and Doug had worked long hours practicing and decorating the area where they were to sing. They had memorized their music, for they wanted their part in the program to be professional in quality. Though Linda had promised she would memorize the music too, she had to use her book. On top of that she flubbed a major solo part and ruined the song. Each member of the singing group was dependent on the other. Those who worked hard had learned the value of persons who can be depended on. This experience also allowed them to discover the meaning of the disappointment that comes when someone you are counting on lets you down.

Tom, Karen, and Doug will have many opportunities in life when they must choose between being dependable or not following through because they would rather do something else. This experience of interdependence will help them understand the feelings of those who are depending on them. It will prepare them for being more considerate of others in their choices. The more roles a person experiences the more perspectives he or she can understand. By being a leader one discovers the feelings and problems of leaders. Experience as a follower, teacher, or one responsible for the safety of younger children prepares one to empathize with others in those roles.

Experiences in decision making and carrying responsibility enhance moral development. They provide opportunities for role-taking and for exercising moral reasoning. Children should be involved in decision making from an early age. Even preschoolers can begin to carry responsibility. The kinds of decisions and responsibilities given to children must be tailored to their capability and experience. A wise mother would not give her five-year-old the privilege of deciding the daily menus. Nor would a five-year-old be given the responsibility of caring for a one-month-old sibling for five hours. But there are real decisions five-year-olds can make, and they need that experience. Teachers and parents must decide what kinds of decisions children can handle and then give them the power of decision making in those areas. When adults tell children that they may decide the adult must be ready to live with the child's choice.

Paul was all set to help mother bake cookies. "Today you can decide what kind of cookies we make," said mother. Without a moment's hesitation Paul fired back, "Let's make gingerbread men." Mother had not thought of that option. She did not have time to make gingerbread men that day, but she followed through with

Paul's plan because she had given him the choice. Next time she wants to let Paul help her with a quick batch of cookies, she will say, "You decide. Which shall we make, chocolate chip or peanut butter cookies?" When the range of choices is limited, let the child know where the limits are.

As children develop and their experiences broaden the areas in which they can exercise decision-making power should be increased. Children may begin by making decisions about the colors to use on their pictures, which learning center they will go to on Sunday morning, and what they and their parents will do when they have an hour together. When children begin to understand rules, they can be involved in making rules at home and at Sunday school. First they will make rules to govern certain activities. Gradually their range of influence should increase until they and their parents or teacher work together in developing the rules by which they live-- rules that both young person and adult can be comfortable with. An important part of setting up the rules will be the process of discovering the reasons for the rules.

Giving responsibility to children has much in common with the giving of decision-making power. The responsibilities should be in line with children's abilities and be increased as they develop. They may start by putting away toys as a parent helps. This is the beginning of a long road toward the goal of full responsibility for keeping their room--and later their own home--clean and neat. Goldfish may be the first living creatures for which children are responsible, but this experience begins to prepare them for the day when the lives of other human beings depend on them.

Once a responsibility has been given to a child or teenager he or she should be expected to fulfill it. Many adults do not shoulder responsibility because during their youth, well meaning parents and friends bailed them out every time they failed to follow through with responsibilities. They were never allowed to learn from their mistakes.

It appears that the carrying of responsibility for oneself and others contributes to moral development. Those who reach the highest levels of moral development are those who have had responsibility for their own lives and the lives of others.

In our discussion of experiences which help persons broaden their perspective--understand an increasing number of viewpoints--we have focused on real life experiences. There are other methods which teachers and parents can use to help children and teens broaden their perspective. Dramatic play is an important way in which children explore adult roles and try to understand them.

Role-playing is a technique used in many classrooms. A situation is explained to the students. Roles are assigned. The students then act out what they think happened next, portraying the feelings and response of the character whose role they are taking. As teenagers role-play a parent-teen conflict, the students taking the roles of the parents are trying to think like a parent. As they get into the situation they begin to discover bow the parent feels, and through this experience gain insight into a parent's perspective.

Drama offers the opportunity for one to "get inside the skin" of another person. An affluent teenager learns the lines of a poverty-stricken youth, trying to imagine and portray the feeling of the words. This teen is discovering a new perspective with both mind and emotions.

In most cases the real life experiences will be more potent than the simulated experiences in broadening the student's perspective. But simulations--dramatic play, role-playing, drama--provide experiences that otherwise would not be available. They make it possible for experiences to happen in a group where they can be discussed.

Time Out!

Kohlberg has noted that persons do not understand moral reasoning which is more than one step above the reasoning of which they are capable. He also finds that persons prefer the reasoning just beyond their own. What should the teacher do about these findings?

A. Discover the precise level of moral development for each student and when talking with students use reasoning which is one step above theirs.

B. Provide students with an environment rich in social interaction so that they will naturally bump into reasoning one step above their own.

C. Discover the level of moral development of the students in a Sunday school department. Assign students of a similar level in moral development to a class so that the teacher can present lessons that are one step above the students' moral reasoning.

The correct response is "B." I hope that was your choice. Much time and energy is wasted if teachers try to pinpoint where each student is in moral development. An environment rich in social interaction will provide the needed exposure to higher forms of reasoning.

What is meant by the term "role-taking"?

A. Making a record of class members who are present or absent.

B. Taking a part in a play.

C. Experiencing the activities and responsibilities of various roles.

In the preceding paragraphs we have been using "role-taking" to mean the performing of various roles (C).

Which of the following statements are reasons for role-taking being important to moral development?

A. Meanings and understandings grow out of experience.
B. By experiencing another set of activities and responsibilities--another role--one better understands the perspectives of persons in that role.
C. The more roles a person has experienced, the more perspectives he or she understands.

"A," "B," and "C" are all reasons for trying to provide many role taking experiences for students or children in the home. Moral development requires a growing understanding of an increasing number of perspectives. Role-taking helps to provide this growing understanding.

Which teacher(s) would you say is/are giving the children the kind of decision-making power that will help them develop morally?

A. The teacher had told the children that they could plan the refreshments for their open house. Proudly they showed her their menu: bologna sandwiches and milk. "Don't you think you should plan for cookies and juice?" asked the teacher. "What kind of cookies would you like to serve?"

B. "Next Sunday," said the teacher, "we will have some missionaries visiting our church. They have a fifth grade boy who will be in our Sunday school class. I would like you to decide what we could do to help him feel welcome."

C. "Here is a new book for our book corner," announced the teacher as she held the book for all the five-year-olds to see. "We want to keep our new book nice. I think we need some rules to help us remember how to handle our books. What do you think we should do to take good care of our books?"

Teacher "A" gave the children decision-making power and then took it away. Experiences like this teach the child that power and position are what count. After a few useless attempts at decision-making they will lose heart and not even try to decide. Teacher "A" is not helping the children develop.

Teacher "B" is enlisting the help of her juniors in deciding how to be considerate of a visitor. If the teacher accepts the children's suggestions and together they work out a plan, it will be an experience that can help the students develop.

Teacher "C" is asking her five-year-olds to set some rules for one specific area of their activities. Most of the children will have had enough experience with books that they will have some ideas about how they should be handled. The task will be within their capabilities, therefore, it will be a good experience for them.

Moving On

Values Clarification

Values Clarification is the name given to another group of exercises designed for thinking about values and moral choices. Many teachers and parents frequently use these techniques The purpose of Values Clarification is to teach the process of valuing. Students are encouraged to think about their activities and choices. They consider whether or not they have other options open to them. They ask, "Is this what I really want to do? Why?" The objective is for the students to consider many optional values, weigh their consequences, and choose their own values. This provides valuable exercise in moral reasoning. As group members share their thinking on issues they introduce new perspectives to each other.

Some Values Clarification exercises are designed to help learners discover what they really do value. The students may be given a list of things or causes. They are asked to arrange the items from the list in order of importance--the item that is most important is placed first in the list, the least important item is placed last. As one is forced to place one activity or cause above another, the person begins to gain a clearer understanding of what he or she really values. Ordering things makes one ask, "Why do I think cause 'X' is more important than cause 'Y'?" Another exercise which serves a similar purpose is to have students answer the following question. "If your home were on fire and you only had time to pick up three things, what would those three things be? Why would you choose those items?"

Values Clarification techniques often ask students to publicly take a stand on value issues. They may be asked to indicate whether they agree or disagree with a certain statement or action.

As we have noted, Values Clarification exercises can provide good experiences in moral reasoning. The discussions which are often a part of the exercise introduce students to new ways of thinking on different issues. These experiences may introduce healthy inner conflict which the student must resolve. The process of working through the conflicts which arise as one looks at personal values and at the values of others can bring about development.

A note of caution, however, is in order. Especially during the teen years peer pressure is very strong. When teenagers are asked to take a public stand early in these value clarifying activities, group pressure may tend to pull the students toward the mean. Those who have low ideals may be raised. Those whose ideals and understandings are beyond most of the students tend to be pulled back to state a position more in line with the actions of the majority.

Another point to remember is that once persons have taken a public stand it is much harder for them to change their opinion. When we state our position we then proceed to defend it. The students' mind will be more open for change if they have not been forced prematurely to take a position.

Values Clarification techniques are specific activities which teachers can use. Because they are relatively easy to understand and use, teachers tend to get very excited about them. This is fine as long as we keep them in proper perspective. They provide exercise in moral reasoning, but they cannot take the place of building a just, caring community in which our students can develop. They should be used along with, not instead of, the other activities discussed in this chapter. Values

Clarification is one facet of experience for moral development, but not all there is to facilitating moral development.

Time Out!

Which of the following teachers are expressing valid reasons for using Values Clarification techniques?

A. Everybody who is concerned about values seems to be using Values Clarification exercises, so, I figure they must be okay.
B. I use Values Clarification exercises because I think they give my students exercise in moral reasoning and also introduce them to new perspectives as they listen to other students share their thinking.
C. The time I have to spend with my students is so limited. Values Clarification exercises are the quickest, easiest way of getting into the discussion of values. So, I use it as my main approach.

Just because "everyone is doing it" is seldom if ever a good reason for doing anything (A). I expect you ruled that one out. Did "B" sound like something you just read? Teacher "B" is using as reasons some of the points which we mentioned as strengths of Values Clarification. What did you do with "C"? The pressure of limited time is something that all teachers and parents face. The danger in teacher "C"s thinking is in settling for nothing more than Values Clarification techniques. The teacher or parent who profoundly influences young lives will be involved in using more than one kind of technique.

Which teacher do you think is aware of the cautions that should be kept in mind when using value clarifying techniques?

A. When Values Clarification exercises deal with personal, sensitive issues I often have my teens work on them privately. This gives them the opportunity of being honest with themselves and not having to worry about what the other class members think.
B. To get a good hot discussion going I make a statement about an issue. Then I ask the class to take a position on the statement. If they agree with it they stand on one side of the room. If they disagree they stand on the other side.
C. I asked my young teens to state whether they agreed or disagreed with the caption on a poster I had just shown them. After the star of the eighth grade football team said he disagreed, everyone else also disagreed. I had the feeling that I was not getting their true opinions.

Teacher "A" seems to be aware of the possibility of peer pressure influencing responses to Values Clarification exercises. Teacher "C" is discovering the way in which key persons can influence responses. Teacher "B" does not seem to be aware of the fact that this approach may be closing minds and making learning very difficult. In most classes the students on each side of the room would spend the class session defending their position. Taking a stand can be a valuable experience in some learning settings, and is the ultimate goal of moral development. However, calling for a public stand prematurely, in the wrong setting, can be counter-productive.

THE CONTENT OF MORAL JUDGMENTS

So far we have said little about the content of moral judgments. We have been focusing on the process of moral reasoning, but Christians believe that *what* people believe is important as well as *why* they believe it. We believe that in the Bible we find what God has revealed about right and wrong. God has given us specific guidelines for living and principles to guide moral decisions.

The structure of the mind--the process of moral reasoning--cannot function without content to process. We might think of the mind and its processes of reasoning as a mill. The moral content--what one should or should not do in a situation--is the grist for the mill to process. If kernels of corn are poured into a mill, the mill will produce cornmeal. If the mill processes wheat the end product will be "Cream of Wheat" or flour. The quality of the mill will determine how the grain is ground whether it be wheat or corn, but the grain--the content--determines some aspects of the final product.

In some cultures anything that is left unattended is considered to belong to whomever finds it. In our culture we assume that toys left in a front yard belong to the children of that home. To take those toys would be considered stealing. The moral content in culture "A" is "it is right to take a toy from your neighbor's front yard if no one is around." The moral content in culture "B" is "it is wrong to take a toy from your neighbor's front yard even when there is no one around." When asked about taking toys from a neighbor's yard children of the same level of development in these two cultures will give different

responses on what should be done, but they will have
similar reasons for their answers.

Time Out!

Which of the reasons below do you think are
similar, representing the same level of moral
development?

___A. My big brother   1. The laws of our
       takes things that   society state that it
       are left around.   is wrong to steal.
       I've heard my   Though stealing a
       dad say, "He's a   toy may seem like
       good boy"--my   a small thing, it
       brother he   should not be
       meant. So, if he   done. When laws
       does it, it must   are broken in the
       be okay.   little things, the
                                    order of our
                                    society begins to ⁻
                                    break down.

___B. My daddy said I   2. If the toy belongs
       could have it.   to a neighbor, the
                                    child should not
                                    take it because he
                                    would probably
                                    get caught and
                                    have to give it
                                    back anyway.

                                    Children should
                                    not steal toys.
                                    Good people do
                                    not steal.
                                    Children should
                                    try to be good

__C.	I want it. Nobody will do anything to me if I take it, so why not? But if the neighbor boy will beat me up . . . well, that would be different.	3.	I would not take the toy. Mother says it is wrong to steal.
		4.	Children should not steal toys. Good people do not steal. Children should try to be good.

Statement 1 does not have a matching statement in the left column. The reasoning of "A" and 4 are similar. The decision to take the toy and the decision not to take the toy are both based on the child's understanding of what good persons do. The reasoning behind "B" and 3 seems to be that what mother and daddy say is right, is right. What they say is wrong, is wrong. "C" and 2 reflect the rationale that if I want something and I think I can get it, why not take it? But if taking the toy means getting into big trouble, it isn't worth it to me. In each of these sets of responses the content of the decision--what should be done--is different, but the moral reasoning-the mental process-is similar. Moral content is important because it does influence moral decision.

Moving On

Moral content--the "thou shalt's" and the "thou shalt not's"--can be used to inhibit moral development. When we give students an authoritarian statement on what they ought to do rather than helping them think their way through to a decision, we have missed an opportunity to help them develop. When we shut off questions by stating the truth with authority, we short circuit development. Christians have a deep commitment to their beliefs. Their desire for their children and youth to come to hold those beliefs is strong. The very strength of our commitment makes it difficult for us to be patient and help learners work through their questions and construct their understandings. It seems safer to stop the questioning by giving the truth.

But God has created human beings with minds that are to explore, question, discover, and be active in constructing moral understandings. If the Bible is truth, which we believe it is, it can stand the questions and probings of our students. If the Holy Spirit is a Guide to truth (John 16:13) we can count on Him to be at work as we guide our students in learning. We will lead our students into the Scriptures and help them discover what God has to say about living, but if we want to facilitate moral development we will not use the truth--as we see it--to whip students into line or to shut off their questions before they have been explored. The Bible can be presented as God's authoritative word while allowing students to explore the reasons for God's laws and encouraging them to be open with questions which trouble them.

Time Out!

In the segments of conversation described below, which parent do you think is doing the most to facilitate moral development?

A. God says we must not steal. It's serious business when we disobey God. Don't let me ever again catch you disobeying God by stealing.

B. You know God has told us we should not steal, but why do you think the One who created us and knows all about us would tell us not to steal?

C. Taking Sally's doll is stealing. God does not want us to steal, so you take Sally's doll back and I'll buy you one of your own.

Parent "A" gave the child no chance to discuss God's law. Instead, fear seems to be used as the technique to bring about future obedience. Parent "C" does not take advantage of this opportunity to help the child think about God's law and the reason for it. The child in the third situation is probably learning "it doesn't matter what I do. It can all be patched up to my liking in the end anyway."

Parent "B" is most likely to help the child develop morally. Was that your choice? God's law was presented to the child with the opportunity to think about the law and what makes a certain action right or wrong. The authority of God's Word was not questioned, nor was God's law used to cut off important explorations in moral reasoning.

SUPPORT

We have seen that we facilitate moral development by the community or atmosphere which we create for our students. We also influence moral development through the experiences and opportunities of social interaction which we provide for persons. The facilitator of moral development has one other important role which should be discussed. Moral development will be enhanced when the facilitator supports the learner during times of questioning and struggle--in periods of disequilibration.

Bumping into questions and conflicts; working to resolve those questions and conflicts. This is the motor of development--the process of equilibration. Without becoming unsettled--disequilibration--without having questions and seeing conflicts, learning and development will be limited. Questioning and the effort to resolve conflicts are therefore healthy activities.

Encourage Questioning

The facilitator of moral development will encourage questioning. Curiosity is an advantage to a learner. Curiosity and questioning can be fostered by taking the time to let children explore and to answer their questions. When adults are curious and interested in exploring questions themselves, they encourage the children and youth around them to do likewise.

A thoughtful, curious attitude toward life will cause young people to question their own thinking. It will also lead them to question the ideas of others and the accepted ways of doing things. Rather than fearing this, teachers and parents should learn how to assist the process. Young people can be taught to identify the key problem underlying a question. They can learn to think of possible solutions for the problem and then search for knowledge and evidence to indicate which solution is best. Parents and teachers can guide this process of problem-solving. They can point the young people to sources of information and provide experiences that will help them discover answers to their questions and solutions to their problems. By guiding children and youth to ask why and explore questions we encourage them to become reflective persons. A thoughtful, reflective attitude toward life seems to stimulate moral development.

The path to a thoughtful, reflective life does not begin by trying to teach young children to contemplate the deep, philosophical questions of life. The wise parent or teacher will lead children and youth in the exploration of questions which are meaningful to them. Questions that grow out of experiences of the learners and are raised by them are sure to be relevant. The adult concerned about fostering the questioning mind will be alert for questions that students raise and will provide opportunity for exploration.

As the teacher or parent guides this exploration, he or she is teaching the methods of responsible problem-solving, and also has the opportunity to lead the learners into new areas of knowledge and consideration.

In other situations the teacher or parent may want to raise some questions which the learners have not discovered. These questions should be in line with the capabilities of the learner. By this we are not suggesting that the adult try to identify the precise spot on the path of moral development at which the child is operating and proceed to match questions specifically to his or her reasoning. The characteristics of the stages of mental development and the levels of moral development provide broader guidelines with which to evaluate our approaches.

Since the same pattern of development is followed by each person we have noted that age suggests the likely level of development. We saw that this is more true in the case of children than for youth or adults since differences in rates of development and inhibiting factors create more differences the older persons are. Most children between two and five or seven years of age are prelogical thinkers. They are not ready to learn the procedure of solving problems in their head, but the attitude of questioning and exploring can be fostered as children experiment with their physical world. They are encouraged to continue asking questions when the adults in their world take the time to honestly answer their questions--even the ones that seem senseless to the adult mind.

From the age of five or seven to ten or twelve years of age, children think concretely. These are the elementary school years. Children are capable of exploring the concrete outcomes of concrete actions. They need exercise in solving concrete problems in the moral realm as well as in other areas of life.

As young people enter their teens many of them begin to use abstract thinking. They become concerned about the feelings and social impact associated with moral issues. Questions related to these areas will be important to teens and young adults.

Time Out!

Which of the following are characteristics of the facilitator of moral development?

A. Enjoys exploring a question and discovering the "why."
B. Uses questions to gain the attention of students. Once their attention is gained, he or she gives them the right answer to the question.
C. Assists students in the search for answers to their questions. Helps them learn how to seek for answers and directs them to helpful resources.
D. Sees questions as open doors to learning.

Was "A" one of your choices? If so, you are right. The teacher or parent who has a questioning mind will encourage curiosity by this example. Did you also mark "B"? Probably not after you read the second sentence. Although a meaningful question is a good way to get into a study session, learning is short-circuited when the adult gives the right answer rather than helping the learners discover it for themselves. This discovery is facilitated when the teacher or parent assists or guides the search (C). "D" is also a characteristic of a facilitator of moral development. A questioning mind is not something to be feared, but rather shows readiness for development.

We have suggested that knowledge of the pattern of development is helpful when choosing questions to introduce to students. Which of the following views do you think is in line with what you have been reading in these last few paragraphs?

A. Students of all ages can handle any kind of question about a situation if they have had experiences which relate to the situation under exploration.
B. Teachers should identify the precise level of moral development at which their students are operating. Questions should be introduced which lead into issues which are concerns of the moral reasoning one step above the students.
C. An understanding of the pattern ˗ of development provides the teacher with some characteristics of the thinking and concerns of learners at the various levels of development. The age of students provides a rough indicator of their probable level of development. In choosing questions to raise, teachers should take into consideration the probable characteristics of the learner's thinking.

Response "A" suggests that the thinking of children and adults is basically the same. The apparent differences are due to the child's lack of experience. This viewpoint is contrary to the understanding of development presented here. There are some kinds of reasoning that a child cannot do. A child's brain must mature before he or she has the potential for exploring abstract questions. We have not suggested that teachers take the approach of response "B." It is not necessary to spend the time and energy required to identify specifically the point of development for each student. If teachers have a good understanding of the general characteristics of the thinking of the age group with which they work, they can choose meaningful questions to introduce. Response "C" is correct.

Work with Natural Processes

The facilitator of moral development will work with the natural processes of development. This will call for patience. Development cannot be rushed. The brain matures at its own rate. Teachers and parents must wait on that maturation process to open up potential for development. Development calls for many experiences and social interactions which all take time. Level two moral judgments should not be expected before the teen years. Working one's way to level three takes 24 to 30 years.

Development is not a smooth and easy road. Periods of unsettled questioning, conflict, and disequilibrium are unavoidable. Patience, sensitivity, and understanding are essential qualities of the person who would walk alongside of another through these periods of disequilibrium. But supporting persons in these times of crisis is a major task of the facilitator of moral development. Let's take a look at some of the things teachers and parents can do to support learners in times of disequilibration.

A prerequisite for this kind of support is rapport with the learner. Adult and young person must have come to know and trust each other before the time of crisis arrived. Communication lines must be open. Unfortunately, relationships are often allowed to grow distant or are never attempted until a problem is obvious. Then it will be difficult to establish the relationship needed for effective support.

Adults who have established an open, trusting relationship with a young person are in a place to hear the beginning rumbles of rising questions, doubts, and conflicts. If those adults understand development, they are aware of what is happening and interpret those rumblings as positive signs of potential development. As parents, teachers, or friends listen to the youth's questions, they encourage him or her to explore them further. The adult listens as the young person explores possible answers and may suggest other related questions which have not occurred to the learner. Since people must work through their questions and construct their own answers, facilitators of moral development will be careful not to hand out pat answers. Some of the questions they raise, however, may point toward solutions. The teacher or parent can also direct the youth to valuable resources.

As we support others in their development, we should never lose sight of the fact that we too are learners. Development is a lifelong process. As we accompany friends on their quest we too can gain a new depth of understanding. The very fact that we are learning, may enhance the learning and development of the other.

Patiently but supportively letting persons work through disequilibrating experiences is risky. When we let them work out their own solution they may not choose the option that we desire. For this reason it is hard for us to "just" be supportive especially when we believe that the outcome is important. We want to step in and enforce conformity, but the price of trying to enforce conformity is high. If we succeed and young people conform without working through their questions, we have stunted development. They are accepting an external standard without understanding it. If we fail in our effort to enforce conformity, young persons probably rebel and go their own way. Now they must work through their disequilibration without the support we might have given. The chances of a negative outcome are more likely than ever.

But if we are willing to be supportive and assist in the quest for new understandings and more adequate answers, the searching young person is more likely to stay with us and consider the suggestions and guidance given. In matters of faith we really have no choice but to assist and not to force, for faith is not real unless it is a freely chosen commitment.

Applying love and justice in our complex, changing world calls for a personal understanding of moral principles. Only when persons have explored, questioned, and tested the rules do they come to understand the principles behind the rules and make those principles their own. Periods of disequilibration are the price that must be paid for moral development. In these times of unrest the outcome of a young person's search may depend heavily on whether or not there is a friend standing by: one who has made the search and is ready to support, guide, and care.

	I have . . .
Experiences to:	
develop reasoning abilities	
exercise moral reasoning	
give meaning to justice and love	
broaden perspective	
social interaction	
role-taking	
decision-making	
carrying responsibility	
simulations, role-play, drama	
Supportive Activities.:	
develop rapport	
encourage questioning	
encourage exploration of questions	
raise related questions	
suggest ideas to consider	
point to possible sources of help	
be a learner also	

Are there things which you have not done that you think you should do? If so, choose one of these activities and plan to follow through on it.

To facilitate the moral development of _____ .

I plan to . . . (activity)

_____

_____

_____

_____

Date _____

2. Barnabas is one of the intriguing characters of the book of Acts. Read the scripture passages listed below and record anything which Barnabas did that you think would facilitate the development of Paul and John Mark.

Experiences	Support
Acts 4:36	
Acts 9:26-30	
Acts 11:20-26	
Acts 12:25-13:3	
Acts 15:36-40	

Let your imagination run a little. What other things might Barnabas have done to facilitate Paul's development?

BIBLIOGRAPHY

1. Values Clarification is explained in *Values and Teaching: Working with Values in the Classroom* by Louis E. Raths, Merrill Harmin, Sidney B. Simon (Columbus, Ohio: Charles E. Merrill, 1966).

2. *Values Begin at Home* by Ted Ward (Wheaton, Ill.: Scripture Press Publications, Inc., 1979), will provide further reading on the subject of values and moral development.

Leader's Guide for Conducting a
4-Session Workshop on "Patterns in
Moral Development"

by
Catherine Stonehouse

Introduction

Patterns in Moral Development has been designed for lay workers in the educational program of the church. It presents a certain way of understanding how learning and development take place. The way of understanding is technically called the developmental perspective. In this leader's guide you will find session plans and learning activities which are in tune with the view of learning and development that is being explored. Whenever we are teaching educational concepts we are wise to "practice what we preach."

Because we believe that learners must be involved in the construction of their own understandings, each session will include small and large group discussion activities. The learners will be sharing and refining their ideas. Learning from other class members as well as the teacher is also important. The group discussions give opportunity for this.

But new concepts are not constructed out of nothing. Therefore, input is planned as well. Reading material is a major source of input. Encourage the participants to read all four chapters of *Patterns in Moral Development*.

In session three you will be leading your group in a discussion of the components which are essential if an atmosphere is to be healthy for moral development. It will be important that each class session demonstrates these components. Be careful to show respect for your learners and their ideas. Be sure that everyone has a sense of belonging and is treated with consideration. Handle questions in a way that will foster openness. Provide your learners with a good model of how they should work with their students.

Let me suggest that you read *Patterns in Moral Development* in its entirety before beginning to prepare for the first session. Then study each chapter more thoroughly prior to each group meeting.

In this appendix you will find copies of the worksheets to be used, suggested masters for making transparencies or posters, and step by step guidance for the group sessions. May the exploration you lead be an exciting one.

A slide-tape presentation is available which summarizes many of the ideas from *Patterns in Moral Development*. This slide-tape set, "From a Child's View" may be rented from Catherine Stonehouse, Asbury Seminary, Wilmore, KY 40390. If you obtain the slides, they can be used with sessions one, two, and four to provide review of concepts from the reading and launch class discussion.

Session One. *The Pattern of Moral Development*

Goals-To guide learners as they:
- Explore the pattern of development in moral reasoning which Kohlberg has described.
- Differentiate between the content and structure of moral judgments.
- Identify basic characteristics of the three levels of moral reasoning.

The Session at a Glance

1. Discussion questions raised by reading and suggested projects.
2. Worksheet completion and discussion. Differentiating between content and structure. Identifying basic characteristics of the levels of moral development.
3. Project sharing.

Your preparation

Before the first session, distribute copies of *Patterns in Moral Development* by Catherine M. Stonehouse to each course participant. Encourage each person to study thoroughly chapter one of *Patterns in Moral Development*, and do the projects suggested at the end of the chapter. All of these activities will help group members to become familiar with the ideas and feel comfortable about discussing them.

If you have an overhead projector available, prepare transparencies from sheets A, B and C found in the back of this book. If you do not have an overhead the diagrams could be drawn on poster board or a chalkboard.

Reproduce for class use worksheet 1 found in the back of this book.

The Group Session

As class members arrive be available to chat about the events of the day. In each session endeavor to create a warm, relaxed atmosphere. Let each person sense that he or she is important to you, not just as a class member, but as a person.

Discussion

Begin the session by having class members share comments and questions from their reading of *Patterns in Moral Development*. Ask: What did you find most interesting in the first chapter of your text? What questions were stimulated by your reading? Be sure that the key ideas of the chapter are reviewed.

You need not feel that you must answer all the questions. Turn them back to the group and let all the learners take part in coming up with answers. Some who have read chapter I *of Patterns in Moral Development* will have helpful insights to offer. While group members are sharing their thoughts you will have time to consider the question, recall what you have studied, and prepare to make your contribution to the discussion.

The diagrams on sheets A and B and the following information may be helpful during the discussion period. Introduce the diagrams as questions are raised which relate to them. You may wish to present them even if there are no questions that directly pertain to them.

The question is often asked, "What difference does Christian experience of relationship with God make in the process of moral development?" The "clamshell" diagram (Sheet A) will help us look at this. The top half of the clamshell represents God's design for human development. God has created men and women to develop slowly through all the levels of the developmental design. God even chose to have his Son experience this same process, and he is the example of all that we were meant to be. The goal of development was to be godlikeness and perfect fellowship with God.

The lower half of the clamshell represents development as we see it in fallen humanity, unregenerate humanity. Since men and women were made in the image of God, we still bear that image and reflect the design which God created, though that design may be distorted by sin. Fallen humanity sets its own goal for development--its best view of humankind. Unregenerated persons do develop morally, some to quite high levels.

We may meet God in any of the three levels of development. We will understand God and God's seeking love with the eye of the level at which God finds us. When we respond to God in conversion we move into a new plane of living with new goals. We move from the lower plane of the diagram to the upper. If we meet Christ while we are working through level II in our moral development, we will become a level II Christian and continue with the process of developing. Becoming a Christian does not automatically cause us to be suddenly advanced in moral reasoning. We need to be involved in the experiences and struggles that cause development. However, Christians who are responding to the leadership and instruction of the Holy Spirit and who have a Christian community which facilitates moral development should be constantly on the move, growing and developing.

Diagram B highlights one of the characteristics of the levels of moral development that we have traced, one's view of the source of authority. The diagram adds another factor, the elements which liberate one from each level and allow for movement into the next. In level I the source of authority is self-interest avoiding pain and punishment and gaining reward and pleasure. Children respond to the external demands placed upon them but for the self-centered reasons mentioned above. As they try to avoid punishment and gain reward they are going through the motions of obedience and through this process are learning what obedience is. When they come to the point of seeing that obedience to external standards is a good way to know how to live and be competent they are liberated from level I and moves on into level II.

At level II persons live by external standards. As they live by those standards they have the opportunity to grow in their understanding of them. Their experience with the standards teaches them that they can trust the source of those standards. As people grasp the principles out of which standards grow and in trust accept those principles as their own, they are liberated from level II and released to go on growing and developing at level III. Obedience and trust run all the way through the process of development. But the dominance of obedience over disobedience is necessary for level II. The dominance of trust over distrust leads to level III.

It will be important to help the learners see why the sequence of development is always the same. Each level of development is essential preparation for the next. We do not discard one level for another. In the process of moving from one level to the next we refine, reorganize, and add new dimensions to our reasoning. We then incorporate it into the new reasoning of the new level. A person is always capable of using reasoning that is a part of a level which he or she has worked through.

Worksheet

Now distribute worksheet 1. Give the class about three minutes to complete the top half of the page. The members can do this individually. For each of the four examples ask the class whether they marked it content or structure. In each case ask why they answered as they did. Statements 2 and 4 indicate structure because they give the reason for the judgment. The others are strictly content statements.

Divide the class into pairs and give each pair about five to ten minutes to discuss the statements on the bottom of worksheet 1. They are to decide what level of moral reasoning is represented by each statement.

When most of the pairs have completed their work bring the total group back together. For each of the five items ask: What level of moral reasoning do you think is being used in this illustration? Be sure to have the respondents tell why they chose the level they did.

Listen carefully to the rationale the learners give for their choices. If their reasons show a correct understanding of the characteristics of the levels give credit for this. When people read snatches of conversation such as are on the worksheet they often read into the statement more than what is there. The point of this exercise is to help the group think about the characteristics of the levels of moral development and not simply to have everyone choose the right answers.

Be careful not to put students down when they do make a mistake. If a comment indicates a misunderstanding you might respond with, "Let's look at that again." Or, "What did some of the other groups do with that item?" Or, "Let's take a minute for review. What were the characteristics of level . . . ?" Or some other appropriate but non threatening response.

Use the sheet C grid to record the key characteristics that come out in the discussion. The grid indicates that each of the items on the worksheet are designed to focus on a particular concept which changes as one develops—one's view of intention, how right and wrong are defined, etc. After a statement has been classified as to its level, have the group tell how that concept would be understood at the other two levels. The following are some of the ideas that should come out in the discussion.

1. *Intentions*

   This is an example of level II. The speaker considers intentions in judging right and wrong. Since the speaker is most likely a child or teenager level III reasoning would not be in use yet.

   Level I—would not be aware of the need for considering intentions.

   Level III—would also consider intentions. At level III this consideration is balanced with a concern for justice. Level III reasoning should not be expected before the mid-twenties.

2. *Definition of wrong and right*

   This is Level I thinking. Wrong is what I am punished for. Right is the commands of adults or what works out to my advantage.

   Level II—right is what good people do or obeying the rules. Wrong is
   what good people do not do or disobeying the law.

   Level III—right is living by moral principles. Wrong is injustice or violating
   moral principles.

3. *Stimulus to right actions*

   The statement represents level III thinking. The person is committed to principles. To be true to oneself, he or she must live by those principles.

   Level II—winning the approval of important persons and groups and the desire to do one's duty to society stimulate right action.

   Level 1—to avoid punishment and gain reward one will do right.

4. *Source of authority*

   This is level II reasoning. External standards are the source of authority.

   Level I—self-interest is the source of authority.

Level III--the source of authority is internal principles. These principles
are internalized through experience with the external standards of level II.

5. *Perspectivism*

Level III is illustrated on the worksheet. The person is considering the
perspective of minorities and the powerless.

Level II-persons can understand the feelings and viewpoint of family,
friends, and one's own society.

Level 1-the person is able to take the perspective of others in situations
which have been experienced.

Project Sharing

Close the session by letting the class members share their discoveries from working on the projects at the end of chapter 1. Several will want to tell of the responses they got from children.

Ask: What impressed you most in the Bible study? The answers to "e" are "content" and "structure."

Encourage the learners to read chapter 2 and do the projects from that chapter before the next class session.

Session Two. The Process of Development

Goals-- To guide learners as they:
• Explore the process of mental development.
• Discover the importance of viewing learners as active constructors of their own understandings.
• Come to see conflict and questioning as positive factors which can stimulate development.

- Identify the necessary factors of development--heredity and maturation, experience, social interaction, and equilibration.

The Session at a Glance

1. Project sharing
2. Construction game--an analogy of how persons construct their understandings.
3. Worksheet--to lead into a discussion of basic understandings of mental development.

Your Preparation

Chapter 2 of *Patterns in Moral Development* will give you the concepts to be explored in this session. As with session one, you will want group members to study the reading material thoroughly and do the projects at the end of the chapter. After doing this study, but before you read your teacher guidance for this week's group session, complete worksheet 2. Then see how your thoughts compare with the comments on the worksheet presented in "The Group Session."

On a transparency or piece of poster board, draw your own version of a "what's it" -- Sheet D. Make it different enough so that class members who had seen sheet D would not be helped to image your "what's it."

Reproduce for class worksheet 2 found in the back of this book.

The Group Session

Projects

Begin the session by giving opportunity for class members to share from their experiences with the projects suggested in chapter 2. Let two or three tell of the responses given by the children they talked to. They probably found that the four-year-olds immediately responded by saying that the large three was bigger than the seven. Their attention will be grasped by the physical appearance of the numbers. Young children are able to call numbers by name and count before they understand the concept of the numbers. The slightly older children will likely choose the small seven as the biggest number. They have just learned what numbers really mean and their minds will focus on the quantity represented by the seven. The older children will say, "That depends. Do you mean bigger in size or in quantity?" They hold the two ideas together in their minds. The purpose of this project is to simply illustrate the fact that persons think in different ways at different stages in their development.

Now let the group share the insights gained in the Bible study suggested at the end of chapter 2. Ask: In these prayers, how many times does Paul make requests related to knowing? How do you think he would feel about the importance of mental development? The responses to these questions will provide a bridge into a consideration of the process of mental development.

Construction Game

One of the most important concepts for teachers to grasp is that learners are actively involved in constructing their own understandings. No one can *give* another person his or her concept of God or a moral value. We can only help other people construct their own concepts or values. The following game is an attempt to give a concrete illustration of how concepts are learned.

Tell the group that you want to see how good they are at drawing a "what's it." Ask one of the class members to help you. Using the "what's it" you have drawn, tell the rest of the class how they should draw their "what's it." Make the rules of the game clear. The person describing the "what's it" may give any verbal instructions which might be helpful. He or she *must not*, however, show the diagram to the group. If someone asks whether or not questions are allowed, give permission to ask and answer questions. If no one asks about questions, do not mention it. After the drawings are completed show your copy of the "what's it" to the class and let them look at some of the drawings made by group members. Move on into a discussion of the experience.

Explain that you want the class members to think of themselves as learners. The "what's it" is a new concept that their teacher--the person who described the diagram--was trying to teach them. Ask: Why are your drawings not all the same? You all had the same instructions. In what ways was this experience similar to the teaching and learning of new concepts? The following ideas should come out in the discussion.

In the drawing experience each person constructed his or her own version of the "what's it." In learning any concept we must construct our own version. Each "what's it"--or concept--is slightly different because of the way individuals interpret the information that comes to them. Sometimes the differences are great. There is a wide range of interpretations of even very concrete terms such as half an inch. Imagine the variation in the images that come to mind when a word such as "love" is used.

Ask: What else might your teacher--the one who gave instructions for drawing--have done to help you construct your "what's it"? Someone will probably comment that it would have been a big help to have seen the diagram. Whenever possible teachers should use visuals. But some concepts cannot be captured in a diagram. To be seen some concepts must be lived. Often helping others build a concept will involve diagrams, living, and many words used in discussion. Questions from the learners are important in building understandings. One of the most important things a teacher can do is to listen to questions and be responsive to them.

Ask: How can a teacher know what the learner's concept looks like? We can look at the "what's it" drawings from our game. But in real life our only clues come from what the learners say and what they do. Teachers must listen and watch to discover progress and misunderstandings. On the basis of what we hear and see we then help students in the ongoing building of their important ideas.

Worksheet

Divide the class in twos. Distribute worksheet 2. Give about ten minutes for the learners to discuss each statement, decide whether or not it is correct, and rewrite those which are false. When most of the couples have completed this task call the group back together again and lead them in a discussion of their responses. Have group members tell what changes they made in the statements and why.

All the statements on the worksheet are incorrect. The following comments will help you prepare to lead the discussion.

1. If a person is a good teacher he or she can *give* important concepts to students. The problem word here is "give." It is impossible for one person to give another person a concept ready made. Good teachers help learners construct their own concepts.
2. Children can be *taught* to mentally organize the things they hear, see, and feel into understandings or concepts, though this is *not a natural process*. In this statement the key words are "taught" and "not a natural process." Organizing sights, sounds, and feelings is a natural process which begins at birth--and

maybe before. Young children do not need to be taught how to construct their understandings. They are born with the tendency to be about this business. In some cases a child's active involvement in learning may have been squelched. When this has happened the child will need our help to begin exploring and experimenting again.

3. The necessary factors for mental and moral development are direct experience and social interaction. Statement 3 is incorrect because it is incomplete. Piaget has identified two other factors that are essential for development--the biological factors of heredity and maturation, and the process of equilibration. Development is the result of a transaction between inner and outer factors, between heredity and environment. Whenever we look at only the inner factors or just the external influences we have an incomplete understanding of the process. Heredity and maturation provide the potential for development. That potential is realized through direct experiences and social contacts.

4. Though most people go through the same stages in their mental development, some *people skip at least one stage*. This last phrase is incorrect. As we have noted, each stage is essential preparation for the next stage. Therefore, no stage can be skipped. Every stage in mental development is important and should be valued. We have also pointed out that there are individual differences in the rate of development and the highest level or stage a person reaches.

5. Each stage of mental development is different from the other stages *mainly in the amount of information persons have learned*. As persons grow and develop the amount of information they have does increase. But this is not the main difference in the stages. It is the quality of thinking that changes from stage to stage. The quality or structure of thinking determines how one interprets

information. New information may create the conflict that causes a person to change his or her way of thinking. Development calls for quality changes.

As you bring the session to a close, again encourage the class to read the next chapter in their texts. When reading has been done in advance this allows for more meaningful group discussions which most people enjoy. The learners will also profit by taking the time to do the evaluation suggested at the end of chapter 3.

Session Three. The Atmosphere for Moral Development

Goals--To help the learners as they:
- Come to a fresh realization that students are always learning from the atmosphere in which they live.
- Identify the components which contribute to a healthy atmosphere for moral development: mutual respect, a sense of belonging, justice, and openness.
- Explore ways of providing an atmosphere with these comments.

The Session at a Glance

1. Project Reports
2. Role-plays--to lead into a discussion of the components of a healthy atmosphere for moral development.
3. Describe a teacher--writing exercise to launch a discussion of the teacher's role.
4. Hints and problems--an experience in trying to solve problems which inhibit moral development.

Your Preparation

Decide who you will ask to be involved in the role-plays at the beginning of the session. If your class is small you could have the same four persons role-play both situations. If there are twelve or more in the class use a different group for each situation.

Make a transparency of sheet E or put the information from it on a poster board or chalkboard. Prepare the cards for the problems and hints activity. In envelopes place four or five each of the green, yellow, and orange cards. Prepare enough envelopes to divide your class into groups of from three to five and give each group an envelope. There should be an even number of groups.

Be familiar with the ideas in chapter 3 of the reading material.

Reproduce for class worksheet 3 found in the back of this book.

The Group Session

Project Reports

Divide the class into groups of three or four persons each. Give the groups five to ten minutes to discuss their experiences with the projects they worked on during the past week. Have them begin by sharing their responses to the Bible study questions. Encourage any who will to tell the other members of their group what they did to try and improve the atmosphere of their class or home. They could also describe the results of their efforts. Make it clear that no one should feel pressured to share if they do not want to.

While most of the class are discussing the projects take one or two of the groups--depending on the size of the class-to prepare the role-plays. Situation one will need four persons. Situation two could be handled by three "actors." Give the description of the role-play situations (worksheet 3) to the groups. Allow the participants about five minutes to decide how they will act out their situation. Encourage them to relax and enter into the acting.

Role-play and Discussion

After the first situation has been played out, ask: How do you think each person in this situation felt? What components were missing which are essential in the atmosphere that is healthy for moral development? For one student there is no sense of belonging. That student would not feel respected by the other students or the teacher--how can I be worth much if no one will even include me in their conversations? If we define justice as consideration for all persons, the excluded student is not experiencing justice. The involved students are also missing an opportunity to learn about justice. They need help in becoming more sensitive and considerate of others. As each of the components of a healthy environment are mentioned list them on the chalkboard. Continue the discussion by asking: What could the teacher do to improve the quality of the atmosphere in the class?

Next, have the second role-play. Begin the discussion by asking: How do you think the persons in that situation felt? How will students respond in the future? What components of a good environment were ignored or damaged? Openness was squelched. Consideration and respect for the student was nonexistent. The student probably feels personally rejected along with his or her comment.

If time allows have situation two acted out with a teacher response that strengthens the atmosphere and thus facilitates moral development. If there is not time for a repeat role-play, ask: How might the teacher have responded to build a healthy atmosphere for development? Examples of appropriate responses are included in the reading materials. Sometimes abrupt, negative comments from students take us by surprise. We need a few seconds to think before we know how to handle the situation. We also need more information to help us better understand the negative comment. It is good to ask students to expand on their comments--to explain why they feel the way they do. This will give additional information and also time for deciding on the next step. Handling negative comments and wrong ideas without rejecting the student and destroying openness calls for skill which teachers need to work at developing. The practice provided in role-play could be helpful.

The Teacher's Role

Chapter 3 of the reading material suggests that the view the teacher has of his or her role will influence the environment. Ask the class members to complete the following sentence: "A teacher is one who. . . ."

Give the class about three minutes to complete the sentence. Ask for volunteers to share their descriptions of a teacher. List on the chalkboard the teacher characteristics that are mentioned.

Have the group look at the list of characteristics and identify those which were mentioned in their reading materials. Are there any items in the list which conflict? If so, which of the conflicting characteristics would be best for facilitating moral development?

Problems and Hints

The teacher who is serious about facilitating moral development must be concerned about the atmosphere in which students are learning. Creating a healthy atmosphere is not always easy. Problems often exist. This activity is designed to help the learners identify some of the problems and begin to come up with solutions to those problems.

Divide the class into an even number of groups made up of three to five persons each. Give each group an envelope of cards and explain the procedure for the activity. Have the steps written out so that the groups can refer to them.

1. Take the cards out of the envelope.
2. On the green cards write problems which you think often cause the atmosphere of classes in the church to be unhealthy for moral development.
   Write at least as many problems as you have members in your group.
3. Put these problem cards in the envelope, seal it, and write the names of your group members on it.
4. Exchange your envelope with another group.
   Do not open the envelope which you have just received.
5. On the yellow cards write hints which you think would help teachers to solve the problems that damage the learning atmosphere in the church.
6. Open the envelope and try to match your hints to the problems that you find inside.
7. On the orange cards write new hints for problems that were not answered in your first set of hints.
8. Groups that exchanged envelopes will meet together and share the hints they have for their problems.

Bring the class together again and have each group report one of their problem and hint sets. As these are shared draw attention to the need for teachers, when solving problems, to be concerned about mutual respect, acceptance and belonging, just consideration for all students, and creating openness. These factors will probably be illustrated in the hints.

Remind the learners to complete their reading before the next session. Mention that there will be a time for discussing their projects again next week.

Session Four. *Facilitating Moral Development*

Goals--To help learners as they:

• Identify teacher behaviors which will facilitate moral development--the kinds of experiences to provide and ways of working with the natural process of development.

The Session at a Glance

1. Discussion which facilitates moral development and project reports to highlight the teacher behaviors.
2. Q sort--evaluation of teacher/parent responses.
3. Contract--commitment to do something to facilitate the moral development of someone.

Your Preparation

Your major preparation for this session will involve a thorough study of chapter 4 in the reading materials. The Q sort will be easiest to handle if there is a table to work on.

Reproduce for class worksheets 4 & 5 found in the back of this book.

Discussion and Project Reports

Ask class members to take a blank piece of paper and list the three teacher behaviors they think are most important for facilitating moral development. Begin the discussion by having several learners tell what three behaviors they listed. Write their responses on the chalkboard. Continue to build the list by asking: Did you choose other behaviors that are not on the chalkboard?

Bring Barnabas into the discussion as an example of one who facilitated the development of others. Have the class members identify the things which Barnabas did for Paul and then for Mark, things that probably helped them greatly in their development.

Acts 9:26-29--When Saul was a new Christian Barnabas supported him by putting his faith in him, accepting him, and trying to help others accept and respect him. He brought Saul into the group.

Acts 11:20-26--Barnabas sought out Saul and involved him in the experience of ministering at Antioch. This was a ministry to Greeks, not to Jews. We can only guess at the significance of this experience on Paul's later ministry.

Acts 12:25-13:3--Barnabas extends his influence to John Mark. He brings Mark along with him and involves him in many new experiences.

Acts 15:36-40--Barnabas expresses his faith in Mark. He does not give in to Paul's opposition but sticks with his support of Mark. Barnabas fades from the picture as he continues to give Mark the experiences which have a part in finally helping him become the person he was meant to be.

Q Sort

Distribute worksheet 4. Instruct the class to tear their sheets apart on the solid lines. The slips of paper labeled "Good" and "Could do better" should be folded on the dotted lines and set on the table as little tents. The learners are to read each of the illustrations and decide whether the adult response was good or whether the adult could do better. If the response was good, that illustration is to be placed in front of the "Good" sign; if it could be better it goes in front of that sign.

When the group members have completed their sort, lead them in discussing where they placed each illustration and why. Remember, the why questions are very important. Look for positive ideas in all responses and do not put anyone down because his or her answer does not agree with the suggestions here. The following points should come out in the discussion.

1. The teacher in this situation could do better. The problem is with the question "How do you think you made Timmy feel?" Steve is only four. He cannot step outside himself and comprehend how Timmy feels. He only knows that he wanted the truck and now he feels badly because he is being reprimanded. Some of the learners may have decided that this is a good response because it focuses on the feelings of others. This is a good point. It is helpful to open the door to development by pointing the child's attention toward the feelings of others. But because of the child's limitations in taking the perspective of another person it might have been better for the teacher to say, "Steve, I know you want the truck. But you made Timmy feel badly when you took it from him. In our class we take turns so that we can all have a good time. In just a few minutes it will be your turn to have the truck. I will tell you when it is time."

2. This is another "could do better" situation. The teacher is cutting off social interaction. We have seen that students learn much from each other as they talk together. This is not to say that students should never work individually. But we sometimes tend to value quiet, individual work more than we should.

3. Teacher number three has a good idea. The children have heard stories about kindness and talked about it. But now they will have an opportunity to actually experience doing something kind. They will probably learn much about kindness from this project.

4. Mr. Green's response is good. He is facing up to a problem but he is involving the students in solving it. He is going to give them the experience of deciding on their rules. He is also giving them the responsibility for enforcing them. We have noted that decision-making and carrying responsibility are two kinds of experiences which facilitate development. Some of the fifth graders are likely beginning to move toward level II in their moral development. Mr. Green is introducing the need for external standards--we need some rules so that everyone knows what is expected. This may be an important new thought for some of the students.

5. Mr. Thomas should also find a place in the "good" category. He realizes that children need something to occupy their attention during a long trip--he is seeing things from their perspective. The discussion gives the children opportunity to exercise their moral reasoning. The family did not stop with the should questions--the content. They also explored the reason behind actions--the structure. These kinds of explorations help foster development. In this discussion children will have opportunity to hear, from another child or a parent, moral reasoning which is just beyond their own. As they are ready for these new ideas they will be attracted to them and begin to move on in their development.

6. Six also represents a good teacher response. The teacher shows respect for the student by accepting his comment as worthy of consideration. A sensitivity to the feelings of the student is indicated by the fact that the teacher did not put him down. More information about the child's reasoning is sought before attempting to offer help. The teacher does not ignore the question and leave the student to answer the question on his own. Instead, the teacher seems to be preparing to involve the student in the process of working through

his question. The response fosters an atmosphere of openness which will make it easy for Jeff to raise other questions which he has.

7. Miss Smith "could do better." Trying to determine exactly where students are in their moral development is an unnecessary waste of time. With children, their age gives us a general idea of where they are likely to be in their development. This general knowledge helps us decide what concepts students most need to work with in the various periods of life. For example, we know that most children in grades one, two, and three are concrete in their thinking. They will benefit from talking about and experiencing the concrete expressions of love. But they will not be able to discuss the abstract aspects of love. Miss Smith would have been of more help to her students if she had spent her interview time in an informal activity where students and teacher could have all become better acquainted. Her story would also have been better if it had ended with a question such as, "Why do you think Sarah should learn to share?" With this ending the children would become actively involved in exercising their moral reasoning abilities. There would be opportunity for them to hear several different reasons and learn from each other.

8. This illustration is meant to go in the "could do better" pile. Bumping into conflicting views and having to resolve the questions that they raise is a process that fosters development. We should not go around trying to create conflicts for children and teenagers, but neither should we fear the conflicts that they bump into naturally. When students discover new viewpoints and begin to question their own, risk is involved. They may discard their former belief and accept the new ideas. If, however, we as teachers are willing to work with our students as they explore the questions raised by the conflicting ideas, we may help

them make their own the beliefs they have been taught. This is not easy, but it is rewarding. We may try to shelter our children and youth from conflicting views. But someday they will meet those conflicts. And then there may be no one to come alongside and support them as they work through their questions. There may be no one to help them know how to evaluate ideas and search for answers.

9. Linda's teacher could do a better job of considering Linda and her needs. Linda is not being treated fairly. She is not having an experience that will help her understand the meaning of justice and love. In the rush of classroom and family activities it is easy for the outgoing, demanding child, youth, or adult to grasp our attention. We need to be always on guard against ignoring those who are quiet and do not demand our attention.

A Personal Contract

Distribute contract forms and envelopes. Comment that you have appreciated the involvement of the class members in the four sessions of this course. But learning must be acted upon if it is to have lasting value. Explain that the forms they have just received are for them to use in making personal contracts. They will fill the forms out, place them in the envelopes and address the envelopes to themselves. Early next week you will drop the letters in the mail and they will serve as reminders of the contracts made.

Each person should promise to do one specific thing during the next week to facilitate the moral development of some specific person or group. Some of the class members may plan to do one of the specific things they had listed for their project at the end of chapter 4. Others may have gleaned new ideas from the group session which they want to implement.

WORKSHEET 1

Content or Structure? What or Why?

Do the following comments indicate the content of moral judgments, the structure, or both?

	Content	Structure
1. Mark should take Kevin's truck back and tell him he is sorry for stealing it.		
2. Sarah should do what her mother says because if she doesn't, she will be punished.		
3. While the clerk was on the other side of the store, the other boys each slipped a candy bar into his pocket. But I didn't take one.		
4. I believe it is important to obey the laws of the land. Laws provide order for living with others. If those laws are not obeyed, the order of society is destroyed.		

Which level of moral reasoning is demonstrated by each of the following statements?

	Level I	II	III
1. Mother will not punish me for breaking the glass because she knows I broke it while trying to fix iced tea as a special surprise for her.			
2. It's wrong to steal because daddy spanks me when I take something that does not belong to me.			
3. "Giving up my seat on the bus had nothing to do with sex roles," explained Ned. "I try to use the Golden Rule to guide my living. If I were carrying as much as that lady and were as tired as she looked, I would want someone to give me a seat."			
4. I know it is wrong to lie because the Ten Commandments say it is.			
5. As I read about the problems of the Indians, I ask myself, "How would I feel if my culture and way of life had been destroyed? How would I react to knowing that most people think of me as a second class citizen?"			

WORKSHEET 2

How Would You Say It?

Read the following statements. If you think a statement is false, restate it to make it true.

1. If a person is a good teacher he can give important concepts to students.

2. Children can be taught to mentally organize the things they see, hear, and feel into understandings or concepts, though this is not a natural process.

3. The necessary factors for mental and moral development are direct experience and social interaction.

4. Though most people go through the same stages in their mental development, some people skip at least one stage.

5. Each stage of mental development is different from the other stages mainly in the amount of information persons have learned.

WORKSHEET 3

Role-play Situation One
Actors: Teacher and three students

Situation:

Sunday school will begin in just a few minutes. The students are in the classroom. Students 1 and 2 are chatting merrily. Student number 3 is sitting quietly, looking uncomfortable and obviously being ignored by the others. When the teacher arrives students 1 and 2 immediately begin talking with him or her. Their conversation continues happily, without involving student 3, until the teacher announces that it is time for class to start.

Role-play Situation Two
Actors: A teacher and two students

Situation:

Sunday school is in progress. Student number 1 is reading Matthew 5:38–42 aloud. Student 2 breaks in with a comment which indicates that he or she does not think the ideas of the scripture passage will work. Demonstrate a teacher response which would damage the mutual respect, sense of belonging, justice, and/ or openness of the class.

WORKSHEET 4

GOOD	COULD DO BETTER
1. Timmy was playing happily with the new truck. Four-year-old Steve entered the Sunday school room, walked directly over to Timmy, pushed him over, grabbed the truck and walked away. As Timmy burst into tears Miss Jones moved in to set things straight. "Steve," she said, "how do you think you made Timmy feel?"	6. One Sunday as the juniors were studying the Ten Commandments Jeff blurted out, "I don't see anything wrong with taking little things that kids leave around." "O.K., Jeff," responded the teacher, "let's think about that. Tell me, why do you think it is O.K. to take the little thing?"
2. The juniors were busily working in their student manuals. They had just read a brief story of a boy faced with a decision. "What should Tom do?" was the question they were to answer. After a few moments of thought Alice leaned over to Pam. "What do you think he should do?" she asked. "Now, girls," interrupted the teacher, "no talking. We all work on our own books."	7. Through interviews Miss Smith has found that most of her class use stage one reasoning when making moral judgments. In last week's Sunday school session she included a story of a little girl who refused to share her toys with her friends. Miss Smith ended the story with the statement, "If Sarah would only learn to share she would have much more fun with her friends."
3. The primary class had been studying about being kind. As a unit project, the children were preparing a little program for Grandma Thomas. She would love to have them come and sing for her.	8. "I'll have to admit that I really wish Scott wouldn't come to our ninth grade class," confessed Jean Stone, the teacher. "I don't like to have our church kids hear his ideas."
4. Discipline problems were increasing in the fifth grade class. Mr. Green faced the class with the problem. "We need some rules so everyone knows what is expected of him," he announced. "This morning I want you to help me make those rules and decide how we will enforce them."	9. Linda was a quiet, reserved child. Ed and Debbie were outgoing. Every Sunday in the kindergarten class someone passed out the treat. Several times, in her soft voice, Linda asked, "Can I pass it?" Ed and Debbie would shout, "Me, me. Can I do it?" Week after week Ed or Debbie passed the treat. Linda sat there quietly.
5. The Thomas family was just beginning a two-hour drive. The children started to scuffle in the backseat. "Who would like a story?" asked dad. In the story Sammy was faced with deciding what he should do. Instead of finishing the story dad asked, "What do you think he should do?" As the miles passed the family explored the various decisions Sammy could make and why some choices were better than others.	

WORKSHEET 5

My Personal Contract

To facilitate the moral development of

_____

during this next week I will _____

_____

Signed _____

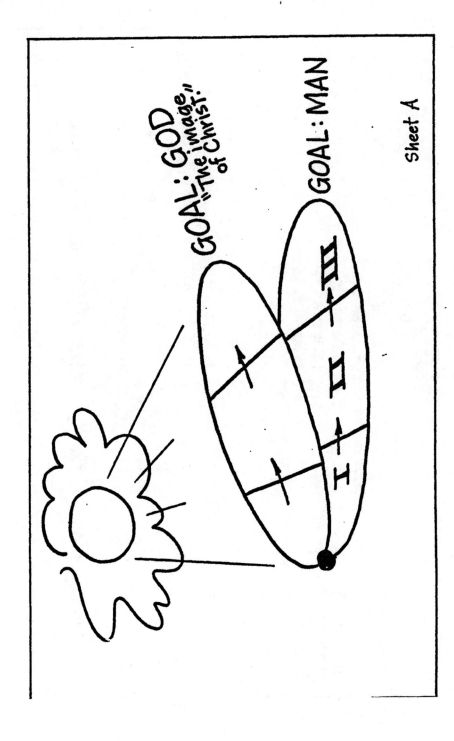

GOAL: GOD
"The image" of Christ.

GOAL: MAN

Sheet A

	LEVEL I	LEVEL II	LEVEL III
Orientation to Source of Authority	assuming self to be authority	authority is recognized as external to self	authority is incorporated into self, as principles from outside having become internalized source
Response to Authority	as to force	as to respected models & laws	as to principles, willingly, even eagerly incorporated into oneself

OBEDIENCE

TRUST

The Liberating Elements

DEVELOPED BY TED WARD

Sheet B

	LEVEL I	LEVEL II	LEVEL III
1. Intention			
2. Definition			
3. Stimulus			
4. Source of Authority			
5. Perspective			Sheet C

A What's It

Sheet D

Problems & Hints

1. Write out problems which you think often cause the atmosphere of classes in the church to be unhealthy for moral development. <u>Green Cards</u> — <u>10 minutes</u>

2. Place problems in envelope.
   Seal envelope.
   Write team members' names on envelope.

3. Switch envelopes with another team.
   DO NOT OPEN ENVELOPE!

4. Write hints which you think would help teachers to solve problems that damage the learning atmosphere in the church. <u>Yellow cards</u> — <u>10 minutes</u>

5. Open envelope.

6. Match hints and problems. <u>5 Minutes</u>

7. Write new hints for unmatched cards. <u>Orange cards</u> — <u>5 minutes</u>

8. Discuss hints and problems with team which has your problems.

Sheet E